Cai Yanxin & Lu Bingjie

Cultural China Series

Chinese
Architecture

Translated by Andrea Lee & Selina Lim

CHINA
INTERCONTINENTAL
PRESS

图书在版编目（CIP）数据

中国建筑艺术／蔡燕歆，路秉杰著；(新加坡)李(Lee, A.)，(新加坡)林
(Lim, S.)译．—北京：五洲传播出版社，2006.11（2007.2重印）
ISBN 978-7-5085-0996-9

Ⅰ.中...Ⅱ.①蔡... ②路... ③李... ④林... Ⅲ.建筑艺术—中
国—英文 Ⅳ.TU-862

中国版本图书馆 CIP 数据核字（2006）第 122186 号

中国建筑艺术

作　者	蔡燕歆　路秉杰
译　者	（新加坡）Andrea Lee　（新加坡）Selina Lim
图片提供	中国国务院新闻办公室图片库(China Foto Press)
	蔡燕歆　路秉杰　张　玲　吴　滔等
责任编辑	郑　磊
出版发行	五洲传播出版社 (北京海淀区北小马厂6号　邮编:100038)
网　站	http://www.cicc.org.cn
承 印 者	北京华联印刷有限公司
版　次	2006 年 11 月第 1 版
印　次	2007 年 2 月第 2 次印刷
开　本	720 毫米 × 965 毫米　1/16
印　张	10
字　数	70 千字
印　数	3001—5000 册
书　号	ISBN 978-7-5085-0996-9
定　价	90.00 元

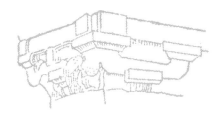

Contents

Ancient Cities

According to existing historical records and archeological evidence, the emergence of China's earliest cities generally occurred during the same period as the rise of the earliest ancient cities in the other parts of the world—at the end of primitive society (3000 BC–2000 BC).

Lewis Mumford, the renowned American city-planning theorist, wrote in his book, *The City in History: Its Origins, Its Transformations and Its Prospects,* that currently, the majority of the known sites of the earliest cities in the world emerged during the few centuries immediately before or after 3000 BC.

These ancient cities were built on a very small scale, with inadequate internal infrastructure, and therefore, strictly speaking, should be defined as "castles", rather than cities, and in no way, could be compared to today's cities. It was not until during the Zhou Dynasty (1066 BC–256 BC) that Chinese cities developed at a faster pace, whereby urban city developments were governed by a specific set of rules and regulations shaped by the feudal system's class ranking classifications. An example of such a set of rules and regulations would be the ancient urban development code, *Zhou Li Kao Gong Ji (Rites of Zhou Dynasty,* Chapter of "Artificers' Record"*),* which contained detailed stipulations for areas ranging from the layout of the cities, to the width of roads for the various levels.

The space layout of the ancient Chinese cities, in the form of the grid system, had its origins in the country's early agricultural society, which was in turn characterized by the "well-field" system (a plot of land was typically divided into smaller square

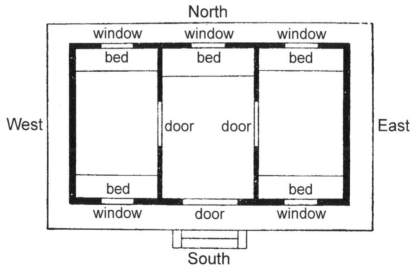

The north-south layout of houses in ancient China.

Riverside Scene at Qingming Festival, *drawn by Song Dynasty artist, Zhang Zeduan.*

plots by the fiefdom chief and allocated to slaves to toil on). On the other hand, the cool northern and warm southern climates of China, led specifically to an emphasis on a building being erected in a position with the front facing south, towards the sun and the back facing north, avoiding the chilly winds. The practice of constructing buildings on a north-south axis, has in turn given rise to the establishment of the north-south direction as the basis of the network of roads.

The philosophic foundation behind the concept of "square-shaped cities" in ancient China was determined by ancient philosophies such as the concept of "round heaven and square earth", as well as the philosophy of *yin-yang*, along with the principle of the five elements of water, fire, earth, wood and metal. The theme of duality featured in the above philosophies led to an emphasis on locating the central axis and thus symmetry, in the basic layout of the cities. As such, many cities and the buildings within also bore names and had locations which strongly reflected their symbolic meaning.

Geomancy *(feng shui)* is philosophy with origins in the traditions of ancient Chinese culture, which held great respect for man's natural environment. Hence, these philosophies had a significant impact on the choice of locations for the ancient cities as well as their layout. Apart from looking at the surroundings of the cities and the topography of the locations, these philosophies also emphasized the planning of the architecture and infrastructure within the walls of the cities.

The changes in the economic structure of the ancient Chinese society brought forward developments in urban city planning. During the Tang Dynasty (618–907 AD), for the convenience of administration as well as to ensure public security, *li-*

3

fang, an "enclosed-structure" system was adopted for overseeing the cities, whereby residential streets and market areas were clearly segregated by the square-grid network of roads. Furthermore, every single street and market area had its own wall and gate, along with a gatekeeper, with the gates opening at dawn and shutting at night. This approach greatly inconvenienced people's lives and also limited the society's economic progress. It was not until the era of the Song Dynasty (960–1279 AD) that the "enclosed-structure" approach to city planning was abolished, due to extensive developments in agriculture, the handicraft industry, commerce, external trade and even scientific and technological advancements. Replacing the clearly defined areas for distinctive purposes, were many commercial streets, marking a shift from the allocation of space within cities from an "enclosed-structure" to an "open-structure". Indeed, one could witness the prosperous and bustling scenes of commercial streets in the capital city of Kaifeng during the Song Dynasty, from the scroll painting, *Qing Ming Shang He Tu* (*Riverside Scene at Qingming Festival*)—classified as one of China's national treasures today.

Capital Cities

Throughout the various dynasties in ancient Chinese history, the rulers of newly established dynasties had always emphasized the importance of choice locations for their capital cities, often sending their most trusted officials to conduct detailed topographical and hydrological surveys, and supervise the actual construction of selected sites. The main criteria for the choice of location for any capital city would be the strategic political and military needs of the ruler. Another critical factor would be the availability of water sources for drinking, farming and gardening, as well as waterways, which were the "lifelines" of every dynasty as they enabled the transportation of grain and other goods to the capital cities. During the 11th century BC, the fall of Shang Dynasty (1675 BC–1066 BC) followed by the rise of

The layout of the Imperial City of Zhou Dynasty, recorded in the Chapter of "Artificers' Record" in Rites of Zhou Dynasty.

Zhou Dynasty saw the establishment of Haojing as the capital city (Xi'an of Shaanxi Province today). The Zhou ruler conferred titles and land upon his royal clansmen, enabling them to build dukedoms in various areas throughout the kingdom. In accordance with this strategy of fiefdom allocation, the Zhou Dynasty began to construct cities which were centers of defense and political control on an unprecedented, large scale. To facilitate the building of these cities, a strict code of regulations for city planning and construction was devised by the Zhou ruler which led to the surge in city-building activities. This also laid the foundation for ancient Chinese cities to be created according to a basic format—the front half of the city was designated as work and business areas while the latter half was reserved for housing and leisure activities. The practice of "taking the middle or central path" had always been advocated in ancient China. Hence, likewise in the matters of building cities and capitals, symmetry is emphasized as the Chinese character "zhong" (which means central). Laid out in a quadrangle shape, the Zhou capital city had three sets of city gates on each side while the imperial palace was located right in the centre. It became the model for the planning and construction of ancient Chinese capital cities. To safeguard their rulers' lives, the capital cities of kingdoms stretching from the Warring States Period (770 BC–476 BC) right up to the Ming and Qing dynasties, had always been fortified with both inner-city and outer-city walls. As the ancient Chinese saying suggests, imperial cities or palaces within inner city walls were built to protect the rulers, while outer city walls and areas were for protecting the civilians. Most ancient capital cities comprised three sets of walls, with the imperial capitals or palaces in the centre, followed by the inner-city or imperial city walls and outer city walls respectively. The ancient Chinese rulers thus depended on this multi-layered city layout to protect themselves.

Chang'an City of Sui and Tang Dynasties—The Most Magnificent Capital City in Ancient China

The ancient capital city of Chang'an (present day Xi'an in Shaanxi Province) was the capital city of choice for the greatest number of dynasties in Chinese history. As many as 13 dynasties built their capital cities here and it was also reputed to be the world's longest-serving capital city with 1100 years' history. Built on a large scale in a strictly symmetrical format, with streets laid out like a chessboard and orderly inner streets, Chang'an was the greatest city of its time. It not only served as the benchmark for other ancient Chinese capital cities, but also influenced the design of capital cities of neighboring countries, for example, the ancient Japanese cities of Heijo-kyo (Nara today) and Heian-kyo (Kyoto today). After putting an end to more than 300 years' of war and strife during the Eastern Han Dynasty (25–220 AD), Emperor Sui Wendi (reign 581–604) began to construct Daxing city (Chang'an city during the Tang Dynasty, Xi'an in Shaanxi Province today) on a large scale during the second year (582) of his reign. Daxing city was built according to layout drawings, after officials had studied the layouts of Ye city (Anyang in Henan Province today), built by the Kingdom of Wei (220–265), and Luoyang city built during Northern Wei Dynasty (386–534). Accordingly, the imperial gardens and government offices were built along the central axis, Zhuque Avenue (which fronted the main gates of the imperial palace and inner city), in the northern part of Daxing city, thus strictly segregating the imperial palace and government buildings from the civilians' dwellings. To the left of the inner city was the imperial ancestral temple while temples for societal offerings and prayers for deities, harvests

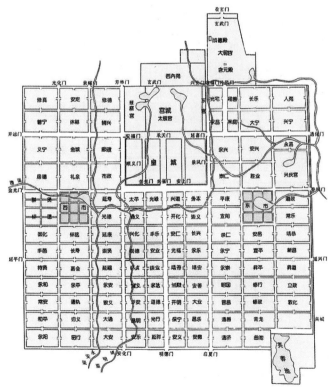

The li-fang *layout of Chang'an, Tang Dynasty.*

and the earth were located on the right. In the year 618 AD, Daxing city was also designated as the capital city of the Tang Dynasty and had its name changed to Chang'an. The city of Chang'an kept to the basic layout of Daxing city, similarly using Zhuque Avenue as the central axis. To highlight the importance of the imperial palace, the streets to both sides of the central axis, the eastern and western markets of the city as well as the residential dwellings and inner alleys were all positioned in a strictly symmetrical format. The city's streets were laid out in a grid system and differentiated by varying grades. The city has 11 south-north streets and 14 east-west streets. Among them six main roads provide direct access to the main gates of the city while the rest were subsidiary roads. All the roads were lined with neat rows of water drainage channels on both sides, and shaded by rows of Chinese scholar trees. The residential areas were further divided into 108 alleys by the road system, where the eastern and western markets were centrally located. For the purposes of security and easy management, all these residential alleys and markets were built as enclosed structures. The alley gates opened and shut at regular hours, and curfews were imposed and monitored by the troops of patrolling guards. There were also patrolling soldiers at night and civilians were banned from going out at night. Until today, the ancient city walls of Xi'an, as well as the sites of the Tang imperial palaces, Daming Palace and Xingqing Palace, are still largely preserved with the original structures of the imperial city of Tang Dynasty.The provision of scenic spots and facilities for the public's enjoyment in Chang'an city, helped set the capital city apart from its predecessors. The well-known scenic tourist attractions in Chang'an included a pond located in the southeast corner of the city and lush gardens. During those days, it was the common practice among successful candidates of the imperial examinations to follow the bend of the river and tour the scenic spots.

Beijing City of Ming and Qing Dynasties—The Symbol of Supreme Imperial Power

With the exception of Nanjing as the capital city during the beginning of the Ming Dynasty, the feudalistic dynasties of Yuan, Ming and Qing, all designated Beijing as their capital city. As such, Beijing completely superseded its predecessors including the capital cities of Chang'an, Luoyang and Kaifeng.

The capital city of the Yuan Dynasty (1276–1368), Dadu (Beijing today), was one of the most magnificent and well-designed capital cities of the world during the 13th and 14th Century. Marco Polo had described in his travelogue, that Beijing was such a beautiful city that mere words could not describe it. As part of their assimilation of Chinese culture, the Mongol rulers had modeled the overall layout of Dadu city after the classic city-planning code in *Rites of Zhou Dynasty*. Apart from the chief architect,

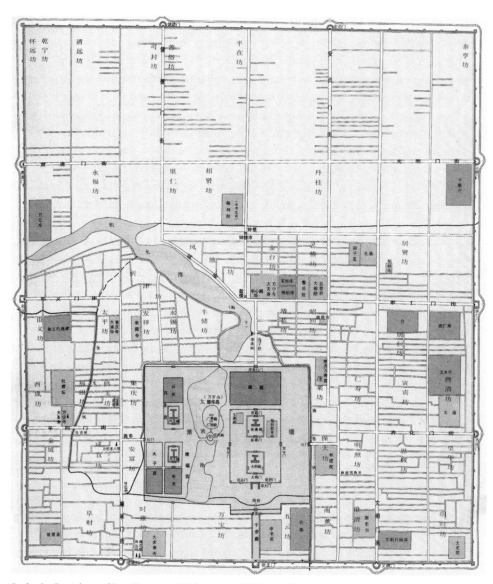

Dadu, the Capital city of Yuan Dynasty in Zhizheng period (1341—1368).

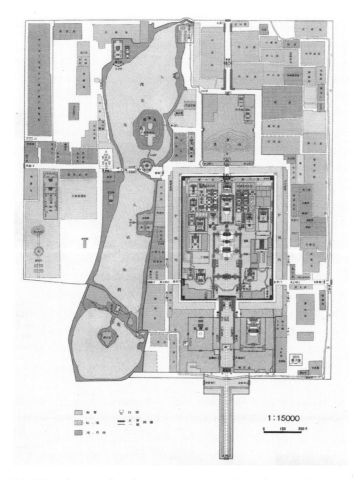

1:15000

0   150   300米

The Imperial City in Tianqi and Chongzhen periods (1621–1644), Ming Dynasty.

Liu Bingzhong, other foreign experts such as the Nepalese architect, Aniko (1244–1306) and others were also invited to participate in the design of Dadu. During that period, Dadu city had 3 sets of walls and 11 city gates, with an orderly architectural layout and a clear network of roads. To accommodate some elements of the nomadic life-style of the Mongols, a piece of land in the northern part of the city much like the steppe, was set aside for the emperor and his sons to practice horse riding and archery. As the original site of today's Beijing city, the locality and layout of Dadu city had a direct impact on the ways in which the latter Ming and Qing dynasties built Beijing city.

Based on the foundation of Dadu city, the rulers of the Ming Dynasty (1368–1644) reconstructed Beijing city. As the capital city of early Ming Dynasty was Nanjing, Beijing city lost some of its importance during that period. For the ease of defending the kingdom against Mongols from the north, the Ming government abandoned a stretch of barren land, about 5 miles wide, to the north of Beijing and thus, reduced the scale of the city. When Emperor Chengzu (reign 1402–1424) decided to shift the capital to Beijing, the southern wall of the imperial city within Beijing city was relocated further southwards by about one mile, to facilitate the extension of the road (for the imperial carriage) leading to the main gates of the innermost imperial palace. By the middle period of the Ming Dynasty, another wall was constructed just outside the southern wall of the city, to ward off the Mongolian cavalry which had attacked from the south several times. However, due to insufficient financial resources, the Ming emperor was unable to construct the other three sides of the city wall to form a complete set, thus leaving Beijing city with an inverted T-shaped layout. The Imperial Palace (Forbidden City) was built at the heart of Beijing city and was conceived by using the north-south axis to bisect the city symmetrically. Spanning a length of up to 8 km, this central axis commences in the south, at the gate of the outer city, Yongding Gate, stretching up north through Zhengyang Gate of the inner city and then through the gates of Tian'an Gate, Duan Gate and Wu Gate of the Imperial City, the gates of Shenwu of the Imperial Palace and finally over Jingshan Hill, ending at the Drum and Bell Towers up north. Built on top of the central axis were ornamental columns, bridges, squares of different sizes and magnificent buildings which accentuated the stately air of the imperial palaces, and clearly emphasized the supreme power of the feudal emperor.

Jingshan Hill, which is located on the northern side of Forbidden City, deserves a mention. It is a man-made hill that was created during the Ming Dynasty, from the soil dug up to create moats around the city. Initially called Wansuishan, the hill was renamed Jingshan during the Qing Dynasty. Jingshan Hill was also the highest point in the ancient Beijing city and its main peak sits on top of what used to be the imperial harem of the Yuan Dynasty. Consequently, the hill was also named Zhenshan, a name with the symbolic meaning of suppressing and preventing the revival of past dynasties.

Beijing city during the Ming Dynasty was strictly laid out according to traditional social norms and etiquette. Taimiao (Imperial Ancestral Temple), was built to the left of the Imperial Palace while the Shejitan (Altar of the Earth and Harvests), was located on the right side. Apart from these temples, other temple altars such as Tiantan (Temple of Heaven), Ditan (Temple of Earth), Ritan (Temple of Sun) and Yuetan (Temple of Moon) were also constructed outside the inner city, in the directions of south, north, east and west respectively. The road network and water system devised by Dadu city of the Yuan Dynasty were retained. The major road arteries of the inner city were the two main streets which ran parallel to the central axis, and connected all the other

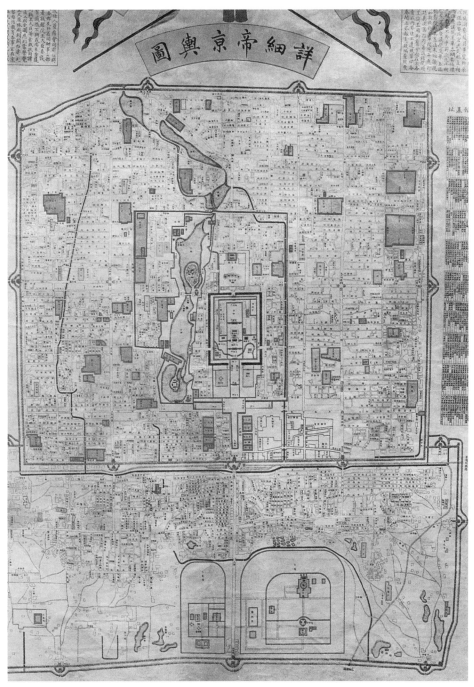

詳細帝京輿圖

The Detailed Map of Imperial Capital, *published in 1908, introduces most of the streets,* hutongs, *and important buildings of Beijing.*

streets together. As the Imperial Palace, Shisha Lake and Xiyuan Park disrupted the connection between the eastern and western parts of Beijing city, traveling in the east-west direction and vice versa was rather inconvenient. The thoroughfares perpendicular to the main road arteries, led directly to the residential quarters, and generally had a width of about 6 or 7 meters. The distance between these streets in turn varied between 50 to 60 meters. This area was where the Hutongs of Beijing city were located

The rulers of the Qing Dynasty (1644–1911) retained the basic scale and layout of Beijing city inherited from the Ming Dynasty. As a large number of the palaces had been destroyed by fires and earthquakes, the Emperor Kangxi (reign 1662–1722) ordered the reconstruction of most of the palaces during his reign. At the same time, changes to residential areas were made, whereby civilians living within the inner city were relocated to the outer city. The inner city thus strictly became the area where the mansions of royal clansmen and the barracks of the Eight Banner soldiers were located. This strategic decision was to lead to the further development of the outer city, where many important commercial areas flourished. Furthermore, some Lama temples were also constructed to promote racial harmony amongst the city's various ethnic groups, such as the Mongols and the Tibetans. The Qing Emperors of Beijing city focused on the construction of imperial villas and gardens located on the northwest outskirts of the city. During the more than 130 years' reign of the Emperors Kangxi, Yongzheng and Qianlong, spanning three generations, they had built a couple of imperial gardens.

The Beijing city of Ming-Qing period was outstanding architectural example of ancient Chinese cities. Edmund Bacon (1910–2005), a noted American architect, had mentioned in his book, *Design of Cities*, that perhaps the greatest piece of architectural work on earth was the Beijing city, "which was designed as the emperor's seat of power, with aspirations to become the centre of the world…that in terms of design, it was gloriously splendid and provided a wealth of ideas for the development of today's cities."

The Beijing city of Ming-Qing period had almost been preserved in whole, up till now. Although most of the ancient city walls of the modern Beijing city had been demolished, the city gates and their names have been retained.

The demolition of the old gates and walls of the city have brought about gradual changes to the old grid pattern of roads. Following the rapid development of Beijing after the 1980s, the newly-built main road arteries of Beijing had disrupted the layout of the age-old grid pattern of streets. Today, only a certain number of valuable and well-preserved architecture including home dwellings, palaces and temples located in the city center are retained as well.

Provincial Cities

Provincial cities had always served as geographically dispersed centers of political and military control for the central government throughout the dynasties. These cities were often local centers of commercial activities and culture as well–amongst them were traffic hubs, handicraft industries and trading ports, or were even a combination of all these positive traits. Factors such as weather conditions, topography, traffic and defense capabilities had led to differences in the layout and architecture of various cities.

Quadrangle or courtyard dwellings were popular in northern China, where most of the terrain is flat. As such, the northern cities were mostly square or rectangular in shape, and had wide and straight roads. The architecture and infrastructure of these cities were also arranged in a cross or T-shaped layout, with the drum and bell towers located in the city centers. The government offices were also always located within the vicinity of the drum and bell towers. Examples of ancient cities with these characteristics include the Xi'an and Pingyao cities.

In contrast, the layout of cities located in mountainous regions with many rivers, was more flexible due to the complex topography. The network of roads in such cities usually followed the contours of the undulating land, and was created more out of necessity than actual planning. Cities built along the rivers were often ribbon-shaped, like Lanzhou, which was built along the river valley of the Yellow River. On the other hand, cities built on mountain slopes, would have main roads which extended naturally along the contours of the mountains, like China's famous mountain city, Chongqing.

The Jiangnan region of rivers and lakes had streets and buildings built along both sides of the river banks, where the waterways were the people's main channel of transportation. The small towns built along the river banks often acquired a ribbon shape while the large towns developed a cross-shaped layout, or a nine-grid pattern that intersected the rivers. The Pingjiang prefecture (Suzhou city today) of the Song Dynasty was a classic example of the city of curvy streets, bridged rivers and plaster walls with black-colored tiles.

Some cities were even laid out in circular shapes for strategic defense purposes, to fight floods or to achieve certain symbolic meanings. As an illustration, the Suqian County in Jiangsu, which was built during the Ming Dynasty, was circular shaped for protection against floods, while the circular-shaped outer city walls of Rugao County (waterside highlands) were its means of defense against attacks from the Japanese pirates.

Xi'an of the Ming and Qing Dynasties

After Xi'an had lost its position as the capital city at the end of the Tang Dynasty, the city's development became stagnant for a long period of time. The city was revived, only when it became the political, economic and cultural center of the northwest region during the Ming Dynasty. The Xi'an city that has been preserved until today, had its foundation laid during the early period of the Ming Dynasty.

Xi'an city of the Ming Dynasty was expanded, based on its foundation as Chang'an city during the Tang Dynasty. It is located in the city center of Xi'an today. The expansion of Xi'an city commenced in 1370 and was completed in 1378. As the higher grounds were located on the northern and eastern sides of the city then, the city naturally expanded in these directions. The drum and bell towers were renovated in 1380 and 1384 respectively. The drum tower was originally located on the north side of West Avenue and was relocated to the center of Xi'an city in 1582.

During the Qing Dynasty, the northeastern part of city was segregated as a Manchu residential area, known as Manchu city. The Manchu city occupied one-third of the area of the city and had a cavalry of 5,000 men stationed there. These men were responsible for suppressing any uprisings of the other ethnic groups from the northwest region.

Despite the fact that a lot of the ancient architecture in the old city had been destroyed over the last few centuries, some of the more complete city walls, drum and bell towers, and temples, as well as traditional civilian dwellings had been preserved.

Pingyao—The Best-preserved County of Ming-Qing Period

Located in Shanxi Province, the ancient Pingyao city was a famed cultural center with a history of more than 2,700 years. Today's Pingyao city can be traced back to the city expansion carried out by the Emperor Hongwu in 1370. It had a land area of 2.25 square kilometers and had South Avenue as its central axis. Built according to the traditional layout for ancient Chinese cities, temples and government offices were located on both sides of the central axis, with markets and dwellings in the city center. The commercial areas in Pingyao city were also far larger than those of most traditional cities, which reflected the economic prosperity of the city. Most of the streets in the city have retained their original names from the era of the Ming and Qing dynasties and were laid out in grid or T-shaped patterns.

Pingyao had been described as a tortoise-shaped city, built with 6 city gates which were representative of its eyes, tail and 4 legs. The tortoise is regarded as an auspicious

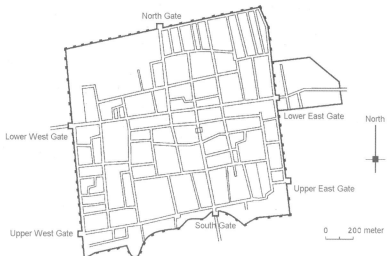

North Gate

Lower East Gate

Lower West Gate

Upper East Gate

Upper West Gate

South Gate

North

0   200 meter

The plan of Pingyao city in Ming Dynasty.

animal symbolizing longevity in Chinese culture. Therefore, the symbolism of Pingyao as a tortoise was meant to bring about good fortune and eternal existence for the city.

Pingyao city has been commonly regarded as the city of three treasures. One of the treasures is the old city walls. The second treasure of the city is the Zhenguo Temple, with its hall of 10,000 Buddhas, built during the period of the Five Dynasties (907–960). With a history of more than 1000 years, the colored figurines displayed in the hall are priceless pieces of art. The third treasure of the city refers to the Shuanglin Temple, built during the Northern Qi Dynasty (571). This temple has more than 10 halls, which contain more than 2,000 colored clay figurines from the Yuan and Ming Dynasties and as such, is reputed to be "the treasure trove of colored art sculptures".

Another interesting historical anecdote about Pingyao city would be the fact that it was the home ground of the renowned Shanxi merchants, and also the birthplace of the predecessor of the first modern bank in China, known as Rishengchang. It was the first draft bank which accepted bank drafts. Under the leadership of Rishengchang, the social credit business in Pingyao city grew with leaps and bounds. During its heyday, there were

The inner yard of Rishengchang draft bank in Pingyao, Shanxi.

a total of 22 draft banks in the region, making it the financial center of China.

Although Pingyao city has witnessed a sea of change throughout the centuries, its basic infrastructure of city walls, streets, dwellings, shops and temples are still in tiptop condition, with the basic city layout intact. It is thus, the most well-preserved ancient Chinese provincial city dating from the Ming and Qing dynasties.

Chongqing—The Mountain City or City Mountain

The mountain city of Chongqing is located on the mountain slopes where the Yangtze River and Jialin River intersect. From the Warring States Period right through to the Qin and Han dynasties, the Chongqing city was already established, with its back towards the mountains and three sides fronting waters. Due to its steep terrain, the buildings and streets of the city were built along various ground levels, resulting in a city which has the appearance of staggered layers of architecture and roads spiraling upwards and around the mountains.

During the early period of the Ming Dynasty, the governor Daiding expanded the city and built a total of 17 city gates, of which 9 gates were "water gates" for the manual transportation of water into the city to comply with the needs of geomancy.

Night scenes of today's Chongqing.

Unfortunately, fires broke out repeatedly and so, the officials shut down 8 water gates to stop "the element of fire from wreaking havoc on their city."

The city gates of Chaotianmen were the largest of all the city gates, and faced the capital city of Nanjing during the early period of the Ming Dynasty. As such, it was the location of choice for local officials to welcome official envoys from the capital city or receive imperial edicts. From the beginning of summer right up to mid autumn, one can witness the turquoise waters of the Jialin River and the muddy waters of the Yangtze River melding together in strong torrents, and creating spectacular whirlpools of water, hence giving rise to the magnificent picture of the powerful rush of the waters of the Yangtze River through the Three Gorges.

Map of Pingjiang (today's Suzhou), Song Dynasty.

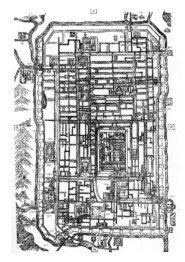

Suzhou—Picturesque Region of Rivers and Lake in Jiangnan

The city of Suzhou originated during the end of the Spring and Autumn Period in ancient Chinese History and was once the capital city of the state of Wu. During the Qin, Han, Jin (265––316), and Tang Dynasties, it had always been an important city of a large scale and population. The city was known as Pingjiang prefecture during the Song Dynasty, and enjoyed great prosperity due to the progressive developments in its commercial

Xumen Gate of Suzhou city wall.　　　*Water Town of Suzhou.*

and shipping activities.

Suzhou city was a highly regulated city, with a rectangular-shaped layout. The city was well protected with large city moats and designed with a grid pattern of roads which were linked together by a network of bridged rivers.

Located in the center but more to the south of the city, were the government offices and military forces of Pingjiang prefecture. As Buddhism and Taoism were equally important during the Song Dynasty, there were many Buddhist as well as Taoist temples located along the main road arteries in the city, thus reflecting the importance of religion in the society. The Suzhou city of the Song Dynasty was also populated with wealthy landowners, scholar-officials and affluent merchants. These people built many large-sized residences with courtyards and private gardens, with even more outstanding architecture created during the Ming and Qing Dynasties. As such, the unique Suzhou classic garden-style architecture gradually developed from here.

Military Defense

City Walls

With wars commonly waged in ancient China, the mechanisms for defense and protection such as city walls, trenches and moats were created out of sheer necessity, but inadvertently led to the development and building of cities. The creation of enclosed cities meant that the most important form of protection were city walls. The earliest types of city walls which were used were simply wooden fences, piled rocks or tamped earth. Before the Song Dynasty, city walls were rarely layered with bricks. However, the invention of gunpowder and its subsequent use in the attacks of cities brought about unprecedented destruction. As a result, some important cities began to fortify the critical defense points of their cities with brick walls. After the Ming Dynasty, brick-fortified city walls became even more widespread. The height and thickness of the walls depended on the defense strategies of the cities. Battlements and watch towers also differed in size and numbers, depending on how the cities were ranked, in terms of importance.

The ancient city wall of Pingyao, Shanxi.

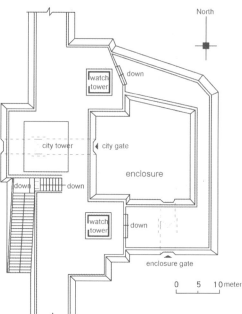

City tower of Pingyao, Shanxi.

The plan of Pingyao enclosure, Shanxi.

(1) The city wall of the ancient Pingyao city

The ancient Pingyao city of Shanxi province has one of the most well-preserved city wall in China, which were built between 872 BC–782 BC. In the beginning, the city walls were made of tamped earth. The city walls then underwent several times of rebuilding and repair during the Ming and Qing dynasties. Today, the city wall spans 6,163 meters in length, with a core wall of tamped earth that was fortified with an outer layer of bricks. It has a thickness of 10 meters at the bottom and 3–5 meters on top, as well as a height ranging from 6–10 meters. The city also has 6 enclosures for defense outside the city wall, a total of 3,000 battlements and 72 watch towers. This well-fortified city of bricks, granite and moats has weathered attacks and natural disasters well throughout the course of the centuries.

(2) The city wall of ancient Nanjing city

The ancient city of Nanjing, which was built during the Ming Dynasty, has been recognized by all as the first brick-walled city of China. The building of the city commenced in 1366 and was a consolidation of the capital cities built by previous dynasties at the same location. The height of the city wall ranged between 14 and 21 meters, while the width of the bottom of the wall was about 14 meters. The width of the top of the wall was between 4 and 9 meters. Altogether, Nanjing city had a total of 13 gate entrances along its wall and every single entrance was double-gated, with a floodgate in front and a twin set of timber doors encased in metal behind.

Nanjing city was the product of the labor and intelligence of civilians from the provinces located in the mid-lower half of the Yangtze River. The manufacture of the bricks for the city wall was of the strictest quality control, with the origins of manufacture and the names of manufacturer as well as the quality controller stamped onto each brick. To further fortify the wall, granite rocks were used to build the foundation and a binding paste of lime, tung oil and glutinous rice mixture were used for sealing and binding the bricks together. This accounts for the sturdiness of the wall even after 600 years.

The multi-layer enclosure of Nanjing Zhonghua Gate. It can hide thousands of soldiers in the caves inside.

Horse-passage on Nanjing city wall. Soldiers in defensive positions could ride to the top of wall in an emergency.

Bird view of the Great Wall from the air. The Great Wall holds a geographically strategic position.

The Great Wall of China

The great wall is one of the most amazing architectural feats and also the largest-scale project for defense in Chinese history. It spans a length of more than 6,000 kilometers from Yalu River of Liaoning Province in the east, to Jiayu Gate of Gansu Province in the west.

The city tower of the Great Wall at Mutianyu, Beijing.

During the ancient times, the great wall was originally built to defend kingdoms against the invasions of northern nomadic tribes. It was Emperor Qin Shihuangdi who was the first ruler to link up all the stretches of the wall into one complete wall during the Qin Dynasty, with the labor of almost 2 million slaves. The rulers of subsequent dynasties continued to fortify and repair the existing great wall until it was finally completed after the Ming Dynasty.

To strengthen defense along the great wall, soldiers were deployed on a regular basis to the great wall and regular repairs carried out. The Ming government divided the great wall into nine defense areas, each assigned with an overall general-in-charge.

The city wall forms the bulk of the great wall, with steps etched across the torso of the wall. It is wide at the bottom and narrow on top with a bottom width of 6 meters, a top width of 5 meters and a height of 6.6 meters. The wall is tamped with earth at its core and fortified with outer layers of rocks and giant-sized bricks. It was said that a line of 5 horses or 10 men could move

23

City wall of Shanhai Gate, Hebei.

abreast, along the great wall at any one time. Battlements, shooting posts and water drainage trenches were also constructed as part of the wall.

The highly efficient practice of using beacon fires as signals during the day in ancient times enabled the great wall to be even more effective as a defense mechanism.

The great wall was not only a project of highly intensive labor, it also reflected the ingenuity of the ancient craftsmen who took into account the topography of location of the wall, and combined it with the clever selection of building materials to create this amazing wonder of the world, that spans the ages across time and space.

The Supreme Imperial Power

The emperor of ancient China was known as the "Son of Heaven" and supreme ruler in his kingdom. The ultimate power and control held by the emperor were symbolized by architectural buildings such as imperial palaces, altars and temples, and mausoleum. These political symbols were the grandest architecture in ancient China, and traditional feudal customs and practices had a great impact on their layout and structure. Consequently, at the beginning of every new dynasty, no amount of labor, financial or material resources were spared in the bids to create these buildings with the most sophisticated technology and workmanship of the time. Hence, to a certain extent, these buildings were also reflections of the highest architectural technology of a particular historical period.

The massive cluster of buildings in which the ancient Chinese emperor resided, was known as the imperial palace and was of a grand scale and opulent style to fully reflect the stately bearing of the imperial family. Indeed, Xiao He, the Han premier who was tasked with building Weiyang palace had the famous saying that the emperor's home was his entire kingdom, which had to be impossibly magnificent such that it could not be replicated, and that there was no further need for the descendants to add to it. His words fully expressed the purpose of architecture as a political tool for serving the needs of the imperial power.

The altar-temple was a unique, quasi-religious architectural structure built for the worship of nature such as mountains and rivers as well as ancestors and famous people. As the "code of conduct" for governing human relationships and actions was strongly advocated by Confucianism, itself a highly regarded philosophy in ancient China, the worship of nature and ancestors was placed under the realm of rites. When Confucianism became an important part of the nationwide culture, and "the code of conduct" observed on a nationwide level, the altar-temple thus became buildings regulated by the government. As a result, these buildings were categorized under architecture for the observances of rites and rituals and exclusively built for the worship of nature and ancestors by the emperor. Examples include Tiantan temple, for the worship of heaven, and Taimiao temple, for the worship of ancestors.

Mausoleums referred to the cluster of architectural structures built as burial tombs and places of sacrificial offerings for the emperors, empresses, and imperial concubines of ancient China, much like the pyramids of ancient Egypt or the Taj Mahal of India. In ancient China, people believed that the dead had simply entered another realm where they continued to live and the dead were basically eternal souls. The rites and rituals observed under the Confucian code of filial piety similarly advocated the idea of continuous worship and treating the dead as if they were alive. Guided by such thinking, the emperors of all dynasties had gone all out to build their very own mausoleums, which were practically underground palaces in the grandest style.

Imperial Palaces

Imperial palaces are one of the most important types of buildings in ancient China. The feudal system in China, which advocated the centralized control of power by the emperor, thus enabled the emperor to exercise full control over his kingdom. As such, imperial palaces were an embodiment of feudal thinking and represented the excellence of traditional Chinese architecture in many ways.

The earliest known palace in China can be traced back to the early period of the Shang Dynasty. The palace which was located in Henan Province, was built on a foundation of tamped earth and bore the layout whereby the front halls were designated for official work while the back quarters were reserved for leisure and living.

The imperial palace of Tang Dynasty, Daming Palace, was built in 634 AD and located in Chang'an city. It was built on high grounds and the most magnificent-looking halls of the palace were Hanyuan Palace, Xuanzheng Palace and Zichen Palace.

The relic of the palace at Erlitou of early Shang Dynasty has a history of more than 3,000 years.

27

Imperial Palace of Beijing City during the Ming and Qing Dynasties

Known as the Forbidden City, the Imperial Palace of Beijing city is the world's largest and most complete cluster of buildings with ancient wooden timber structures today. Built by the Emperor Yongle of the Ming Dynasty in 1406 and completed in 1420, a total of 24 emperors ascended the throne in this palace. Another name, The Forbidden City, is so-called because it was forbidden for the commoner to enter the compound on pain of death. It was also forbidden for any building in Beijing to be constructed higher then the buildings in the Forbidden City. The yellow color of the tiled roofs could not be used by commoners.

The Imperial Palace was built right in the centre of Beijing city, following the importance of the central position as the seat of supreme power, in accordance with traditional Chinese thinking. All the imperial buildings had walls which were painted red, and yellow glazed-tiled roofs, providing a stark contrast against the drab grey tiles of residential dwellings outside the imperial palace.

The Imperial Palace occupies a space area of 720,000 square meters and is made of more than 9,000 buildings. It is thus the cluster layout of the palace which makes it unique, when compared to other architectural wonders of the world, such as the Louvre Palace and Versailles Palace of France.

The Imperial Palace is surrounded by moats, towers and several gates, with the main gate of Wu, being the most outstanding. The walled area of the Forbidden City serves as the residence and office of the Imperial family and their household staffs, as well as the offices of the ministers and favored officials. The whole compound has some nine thousand rooms capable of housing the imperial family, administrators, eunuchs, maids and soldiers.

Most structures are of wood, and hence prone to fire. The foundation is of stone and the roofs of yellow glazed tiles. The city is surrounded at its boundary by a ten meter high red wall and a fifty meter wide moat. An exemption to imperial yellow tiling was for the library where the tiles were black to symbolize water and capable of suppressing fire. Each imperial door has nine rows of nine knobs, a total of 81, as an imperial designation that the number nine is an imperial number. The dragons all have five claws to as an imperial symbol. Commoners using the nine knobs and the five dragon claws faced execution.

The layout of the Forbidden City with its six main axial buildings is very simple. The front is the southern entrance and one enters the main attractions facing northwards. On a north-south axis, the compound is divided into two complexes, the southern outer courtyard with three principal halls (Taihe Hall, Zhonghe Hall and Baohe Hall), and northern inner courtyard of another three main buildings made up

The Map of Ming Capital City *depicts the panorama of the Forbidden City in the Ming Periods. The character dressing in government official attire depicted in the bottom right corner of the picture is Kuai Xiang, the designer of the Imperial Palace in Beijing.*

29

Turret of the Imperial Palace.

of two palaces and one hall (Qianqing Palace, Jiaotai Palace and Kunning Palace). The administrative area is the larger southern outer sector and the private quarters are to the smaller northern inner sector. Secondary halls and palaces are to both sides of this central axis.

The Forbidden Palace starts at Tian'an Gate passing northwards to Wu Gate or Meridian Gate, a giant gate with five pavilions guarding the main entrance to the compound. Wu Gate, also known as the Gate of Five Phoenixes, has played an important site in Ming and Qing history. It was the site of official imperial announcements of the Chinese calendar, the inspections of troops by the Emperor and the execution or pardon of prisoners at his behest. The Wu Gate has three doors, the central one only for the Emperor, the Empress (if in a sedan) as well as once in a lifetime for the top three scholars of the imperial exam.

Immediately past the Wu Gate are five marble bridges over a small stream called the Jinshuihe (Gold Water Steam) leading to a large outer courtyard guarded by a smaller gateway, the Taihe Gate, at the entrance of its corresponding Taihe Hall. The Taihe Hall and following two halls are each guarded at the entrance by a gate of the same name. These gates (Taihe Gate, Zhonghe Gate and Baohe Gate) are thus followed by their corresponding halls, viz. Taihe Hall, Zhonghe Hall and Baohe Hall.

The Taihe Hall (Hall of Supreme Harmony) is the tallest and largest of the buildings for the most important imperial banquets and ceremonies, such as the ascendance to the throne, the First day of the New Year, the Winter Solstice and the Emperor's Birthday. Prior to the Qianlong period, it was also where the imperial exams were held and the results announced. The hall has a raised golden lacquered throne between two dragon decorated pillars and under a sphere hanging form a colorful carved ceiling. A nine dragon screen behind the throne symbolizes longevity and the unity of heaven and earth. One can see gargoyles of dragon and tortoise parts, said to show immortality and longevity. A grain measure and a sundial reflect on imperial justice and righteousness while a large gold plated copper cauldron was filled with water to be used for any fire. Bronze tripods were for incense and cranes again indicate longevity.

Further north is the smallest hall called Zhonghe Hall (Hall of Central Harmony) where the Emperor made his private preparations in donning his regalia before proceeding to Taihe Hall. This was also where the Emperor inspected the grain for annual planting, communicate with his entire family (sometimes including his numerous concubines), and receiving foreign dignitaries.

Beyond Zhonghe Hall is the Baohe Hall (Hall of Preserving Harmony) for smaller banquets, ceremony and imperial exams during and after the Qianlong period. The successful candidates were awarded the scholar title. The rooms have been converted as a museum to display the Imperial treasures and gifts from foreign rulers.

Still proceeding northwards one then enters the Qiangqing Palace (Palace of Heavenly Purity) through the Qianqing Gate (Gate of Heavenly Purity). This was the residence of the Ming and early Qing Emperors. This was where the last Ming Emperor killed his young daughter and his concubines before hanging himself at Coal Hill. In front of this palace are bronze tortoises and cranes, a grain measure and a sundial. At the door is a tablet with calligraphy words "Sincerity and Openness" by the Shunzhi Emperor who abdicated in favor of Kangxi to be a Buddhist monk. The throne is again accompanied by a dragon screen behind it, and the ceiling is spectacular.

Further north of the Qianqing Palace is Jiaotai Hall (Hall of Union) with its beautiful ceiling and the twenty-five imperial seals of the Qianlong Emperor and a chiming clock and a clepsydra or water clock. (The Chinese had invented their own clepsydra prior to the Song Dynasty). After Jiaotai Hall is Kunning Palace (Palace of Earthly Tranquility) where the Ming Empresses lived. This was where the last Ming Empress

Taihe Hall of the Forbidden City in Beijing.

hanged herself. It was converted to a Qing sacrificial chamber but became the bridal chamber of Henry Puyi, the last emperor of China, with the double character *xi* to indicate happiness and fertility.

To east of Taihe Gate is Wenyuan Hall (Hall of Literary Glory) previously house of Ming crown prince but converted to a meeting place for the emperor and his scholars. During the Qianlong period it was made into the imperial library of 36,000 volumes. To west of Taihe Gate is Wuying Hall (Hall of Martial Spirit) initially for Ming Emperors to rest during fasting period. During Kangxi reign it was the site for compilation of the Kangxi Dictionary. Once past the Qianqing Gate (Gate of Heavenly Purity) leading to the Qianqing Palace (Palace of Heavenly Purity) is the inner court which is located the Imperial family chambers previously housing thousands of women and eunuchs. To the east of Qianqing Palace is Zhai Palace, which is a is a museum for bronze objects, and Ningshou Palace where Qianlong lived after his abdication and it now houses paintings and art objects.

The imperial flower garden, with rocks, pond, bamboo, flowers, fir and cypress trees and pavilions is located at the north end of the compound behind the Kunning Palace. Landscaped during the Ming Dynasty, it covers 7,000 square meters. On the Double Nine Festival, the imperial family would ascend the Yujing Pavilion (Imperial Viewing Pavilion) to view and relax. To the east is the Hall of Literary Elegance where rare classical books were kept.

It is not enough to see the Forbidden City in one morning or afternoon as on the usual tourist itinerary. For those who want to enjoy Chinese art and beauty, the Forbidden City requires a second longer and more elaborate visit. At such a time look closely at the roofs (ten mythological animals at the Hall of Supreme Harmony) and the wall and ceiling decors, reflect on the imperial history behind each hall, understand the animals symbolic of Chinese beliefs such as the lions, the crane, tortoise and dragons, and take the time to see the art pieces and the paintings.

Shenyang Imperial Palace of the Qing Dynasty

With an area of 60,000 square meters, about one twelfth the size of the Forbidden City, the Shenyang Imperial Palace differs primarily from its better known Beijing counterpart on account of its history, Manchu-style architecture and unique local geographical conditions.

The Manchurian influence behind its construction is also a vast departure from

Dazheng Hall of Shenyang's Imperial Palace, Qing Dynasty.

33

the style of its predecessor.

Construction began when Nurhachi was in power and was completed in 1636 by his son, Abahai (Huangtaiji), the grandfather of Shunzhi, later to become the first emperor of China's last feudal empire, the Qing Dynasty (1644–1911).

The imperial palace is distinctive for the Manchu-style architecture blended with Han and Mongolian influences. The main structure includes three sections. The eastern section is probably the most impressive for the octagonal Dazheng Hall, The Hall of Great Affairs, in vivid red and gold, inside which is an elaborate throne where Shunzhi was crowned.

The middle section starts at Daqing Gate, the Main Gate, behind which is the grand Chongzheng Hall (Hall of Supreme Administration), where Abahai commanded military affairs and conducted daily business. The emperor also met diplomats from abroad and leaders of minority groups in this hall.

Behind the hall, there is a route leading to the Fenghuang Tower (Phoenix Tower) and the study of Abahai. It was noted as Shenyang's highest building at that time.

At the rear of the middle section is the Qingning Palace, The

The garden of Qing's Imperial Palace in Shenyang.

Palace of Pure Tranquility and the bed chamber for Abahai and his mistress.

The western section was added in 1782 by Emperor Qianlong (reign 1736–1795), and its main building is the Wenshuo Hall (Hall of Literary Source), which contains the complete works of the Four Treasures as well as a copy with the inscription of Emperor Qianlong.

Temples and Altars

Tiantan (The Temple of Heaven)—Sacred Altar of Heaven

The pole on which meat was feed to crows as sacrifice in Shenyang's Imperial Palace.

The Temple of Heave was established in 1420 during the reign of Ming Emperor Yongle (reign 1403–1424), who also founded the Forbidden City. The temple was originally established as the Temple of Heaven and Earth, but was given its current name during the reign of Ming Emperor Jiajing (reign 1522–1567), who built separate complexes for the earth, sun, and moon. The architecture and layout of the Temple of Heaven is based on elaborate symbolism and numerology. In accordance with principles dating back to pre-Confucian times, the buildings in the Temple of Heaven are round, like the sky, while the foundations and axes of the complex are rectilinear, like the earth. The symbolism of the temple was necessary since the complex served as the setting in which the Emperor, the Son of Heaven, directly beseeched Heaven to provide good harvests throughout the land. This was important since agriculture was the foundation of China's wealth in the imperial period. Since the ceremony at the Temple of Heaven was thought to directly affect the people's livelihood, news of the ceremony each year was disseminated throughout China.

The original function of Temple of Heaven was to provide a place for the emperors of Ming and Qing dynasties to pray for rain and a good harvest. The emperor came to the Temple of Heaven twice a year to pray. The first time was to pray for rain and good harvest and the second was to worship God by offering sacrifice. The first time was the 15th of the first month of the

Chinese Architecture

The Ancestral Temple of Marquis Wu in Chengdu, Sichuan.

Chinese Lunar year (usually between January 20 and February 20). Qinian Hall (Hall of Annual Prayer) was where the final rite took place. Built in 1420, it is 38 meters high and 32.72 in diameters. The style of the architecture bore ancient Chinese philosophy which was that the Heaven dominated the world. The emperor arrived at the Temple of Heaven from the Forbidden City one day before the rite. He first burned some joss sticks in the Huang Qiong Yu (Imperial Vault of Heaven) and then had the name cards of the divinities moved to the Hall of Prayer for Good Harvests. After that he went to the imperial kitchen to check if all the sacrifice for the rite were prepared. Next morning, the rite began at four o'clock. The emperor went out of Hall of Abstinence to Ju Fu Tai where the emperor dressed up. Then he was accompanied by the ministers and relatives to the Hall of Prayer for Good Harvests. The emperor fell on his knees and kowtowed nine times to the name cards of the divinities. At this time, the stoves beside the Hall of Prayer for Good Harvests were burned. Music was a must. The band started to play music while dancers were dancing.

The second time of the year for pray was on the midwinter day (December 22). This time was to worship God by offering sacrifice. The rite took place on the Huan Qiu (Circular Mound Altar). During the days of rite, the emperor strictly abstained from many things. No meat, no alcohol, no entertainment, no condolence, no politics and no concubines. The Circular Mound Altar sits at the southern end of the Temple of Heaven. This empty three-tiered plinth that rises from a square yard was constructed in 1530 and rebuilt in 1740 and it is built of white marble.

Next along the axis are the Echo Wall and the Imperial Vault of Heaven. The echo wall, 193.2 meters around, 0.9 meter thick and 61.5 meters in diameter, named for its acoustical properties, permits a whisper spoken at one end to be heard from the other. The Triple Echo Stones in the courtyard return various numbers of echoes depending on the stone one stands on. The acoustics

The main buildings of the Temple of Heaven– the Circular Mound Altar, the Imperial Vault of Heaven, Hall of Annual Prayer are on the same north-south axis.

Hall of Annual Prayer in the Temple of Heaven.

37

The Circular Mound Altar is one of the main buildings of the Temple of Heaven and the place where ancient emperors held the rite of Heaven worship.

The Imperial Vault of Heaven, built in 1530.

were used in ancient Chinese architecture. The Imperial Vault of Heaven, which sits in the center of the plaza, is a round building that once contained memorial tablets of the Emperor's ancestors.

Some other sites such as Dan Bi Qiao (Bridge of Vermilion Stairway), Zai Sheng Ting (Butcher Pavilion) and Long Corridor are also the attached facilities for the rite.

Shejitan—Altar of the Earth and Harvests

The Altar of the Earth and Harvests in Zhongshan Park (Sun Yat-sen Park) in the centre of Beijing was where the emperors of the Ming and Qing Dynasties held grand ceremonies, from the 14th until the early 20th century, to offer sacrifices to the God of the Earth and the God of Harvests. The altar's name in Chinese is *she-ji-tan*, wherein *she* means the God of the Earth, *ji* the God of the Five Common Cereals, that is, rice, maize, millet, wheat and beans. The earth and the cereals sustain the life of human beings and hence ceremonies were held to pay respect to them.

The Altar of the Earth and Harvests, which sits at the intersection of its two axes, is the centerpiece structure of Sun Yat-sen Park. Square in shape, the altar consists of three tiers, with the top tier 16 meters on each side, the second 16.8metres and the base 17.8metres.Constructed of white marble, it looks majestic and dignified, In accordance with the traditional philosophy that there are five basic elements in life, namely, metal, wood, water, fire and earth, the designer had the surface of the top tire divided into five areas, each filled with hard-packed earth of a particular color, yellow in the middle, green to the east, white to the west, red to the south and black to the north. Such a design signified the rule of the emperor over all the five regions under heaven each of which was represented by a particular color.

As the national capital in the Ming and Qing dynasties, Beijing understandably has the most magnificent Altar of the Earth and Harvests ever constructed in the land. According to historical archives, when the imperial palace was being built during the reign of Emperor Chengzu of Ming (reign 1403–1425), an Altar of the Earth and Harvests was erected on a former temple located west of today's Tian'an Gate. The sitting was in accordance with the principle that "the ancestral temple should be located on the left-hand side (east) of the palace while the Altar of the Earth and Harvests should be on the right-hand side (west)." Since that day, the altar had been in use until the overthrow of the Qing Dynasty and this is the altar we see today in Sun Yat-sen Park.

In Ming and Qing, there used to be in the yellow-earth section in the middle of the Altar of the Earth and Harvests a shrine, square in shape, in which were housed two steles, one made of stone and the other of wood, about 1.2 meters tall each and half a meter each side. These were the spirit tablets of the God of the Earth and the God of Harvests respectively. While the stone one was weather-proof, the wooden stele would start rotting in time and had to be replaced from time to time. Whenever this was done, people would say in joke, "Ah, the God of the Earth is

Shejitan (Altar of the Earth and Harvests, now Beijing Zhongshan Park), originally built in 1421, was where the Ming and Qing emperors offered sacrifice to the God of Earth and the God of Harvests.

going to have a new bride again." When the story came to the ear of Emperor Qianlong, he thought it irreverent and sacrilegious to make jokes about the gods and so issued a decree to have the wooden stele removed for good and all and leave only the stone one. In 1950, the stone one was also removed with the result that now only the five-colored earth, left from the days of Ming and Qing, is seen on the altar.

In the past, on the two occasions of the summer solstice and the winter solstice, the reigning emperor would come to the altar and pay homage and offer sacrifices to the God of the Earth and the God of Harvests. The ceremony was held in the open, rain or shine. Later a hall was built to the north of the altar where the emperor could take a rest or conduct the ceremony when it rained or snowed.

Taimiao (Imperial Ancestral Temple)—Place for Emperors to Offer Sacrifices to Their Ancestors

The Imperial Ancestral Temple was originally built in 1420 under the Ming Dynasty and is located just southeast of the Forbidden City. This ornate temple complex stuns the eye and the senses with an atmosphere that can best be described as somewhat unreal, beyond time and history.

During the Ming and Qing dynasties, on occasions such as an emperor's ascending the throne, a triumphant return from battle or the presentation of prisoners of war, the emperor would first come here to offer sacrifices to his ancestors. At other times, the huge temple stood empty except for the few bailiffs who guarded the doors and a great flock of gray cranes. The temple remained in this state for the netter part of more than 500 years until International Labor Day in 1951, when it became the Beijing Working People's Cultural Palace.

The central part of the Imperial Ancestral Temple consists of three magnificent halls, each with its own auxiliary halls. The front hall, the largest of the three, has a double-eaved roof and tests on a three-layer stone base. Before it to the south is a spacious courtyard with long corridors enclosing it on each side. At the southern end of the courtyard is a compound with a pavilion

and several exquisite stone bridges spanning the Jinshuihe (Golden River). A forest of ancient cypress trees surrounds these buildings, which, with their strong yet simple style, from a single integrated whole with the Imperial Palace.

The Front Hall of the Imperial Ancestral Temple.

Imperial Mausoleums

A total of 50–60 dynasties were founded through out Chinese history, made up of either unified kingdoms under one emperor or separated regimes under the rule of feudal lords. Those in power were all buried in majestic mausoleums after they had died (in fact, many of them began to build their very own mausoleums right from the moment they ascended the throne). According to statistics, there are an estimated 300 to 400 imperial mausoleums located all over China's more than ten provinces, municipalities, and autonomous regions.

The ancient burial rites of China during the remote ages were very simple. However, by the period of Shang Dynasty, a great emphasis was place on burial rites and rituals, which was then included in the rites of the imperial court. From then on, grand burial rites and rituals become the common practice among future rulers.

Most mausoleums comprised structures which were locate underground as well as above ground. Located underground were tomb chambers which contained the coffins. Initially wooden structures, these chambers later evolved into structures built with bricks and rock. During the Qin Dynasty, massive structures were built for the mausoleums with highly intensive labor. Planted on top were rows and rows of cypress trees as a symbolic representation of the mountain forest. The ancient Chinese emperor's tomb was commonly known as "the emperor's final resting place", or "mountain mound", a homonym of the Chinese phrase for mountain forest, hence the origin of the tree-planting practice. During the Tang Dynasty, the emperors' tombs were often built by directly excavating hills. Above the ground, the architectural layout surrounding the actual tombs was often comprehensively planned, including the topography, the entrances to the mausoleums, passageways for gods, sacrificial altars and greenery.

Due to the long passage of time, many of the underground chambers of these mausoleums had mostly been looted. The mausoleums, which more or less retained their form were the imperial mausoleums built during the Ming and Qing dynasties. The Qing and Ming imperial mausoleums are also the most sophisticated and outstanding examples of ancient Chinese imperial mausoleum architecture.

Qin Mausoleum—Mysterious Underground Kingdom

The Qin Mausoleum, located in Lintong County, Shaanxi Province, is surrounded by the Lishan Mountains to the south and the Wei River to the north. Such a location coincides the traditional Chinese geomantic omens because the site, surrounded by mountains and rivers, was an ideal burial site for feudal emperors who believed they would lead a new life in another world.

Construction of the Qin Mausoleum, the largest imperial tomb in China, began in 247 BC soon after Qin Shihuangdi ascended to the throne and was still underway at his death in 210 BC. Construction of auxiliary projects was halted in 208 BC when troops surrounded the imperial capital during an uprising.

Numerous groups of people worked on the 39-years construction project, from high-ranking officials such as Prime Minister Li Si who was in charge of the work, to criminals forced to do manual labor. As many as 720,000 workers from across the country helped construct the tomb.

Criminals were forced to cut and transport massive logs from a thousand miles away, as well as large stones from hundreds of miles distant. Numerous laborers died from hard labor carried out for many years. The unmatched immense magnificent mausoleum represents a solemn, but nonetheless stirring segment in the history of China.

The mausoleum, which covers 56.25 square kilometers, was designed in accordance with the layout of the emperor's capital. The original tomb, measuring some 120 meters in height, was covered with dirt. The remaining 50 meters of the structure resemble a topless pyramid. A city wall, measuring four meters in height and four meters in width, encircles the buried palace. The wall, constructed of unfired bricks, has gates on four sides.

The tomb was originally surrounded by two rectangular walls some eight meters thick, with the outer wall stretching 6,264 meters and the inner 3,870 meters. Both walls featured comer towers and broad gates on four sides, with the arrangement

The Mausoleum of Emperor Qin Shihuangdi.

Pit 1 of Emperor Qin Shihuangdi's Terra-cotta Museum.

resembling a real city. Pieces of tile, gate stones and piles of red soil are all that remain of the once magnificent structure. High walls, measuring one meter in height, located at the southern end of the tomb complex. The sections allow one to clearly see the denseness of layers which are between five and seven centimeters thick. The thick flat loam walls, which are strong as bricks, represent the wonderful craftsmanship found thousands of years ago.

Life size terra-cotta figures of warriors and horses arranged in battle formations are the star features at the Qin Mausoleum. They are replicas of what the imperial guard should look like in those days of pomp and vigor. Altogether over 7,000 pottery soldiers, horses, chariots, and even weapons have been unearthed from these pits. Most of them have been restored to their former grandeur.

Hundreds of auxiliary tombs, both large and small, have been found inside and outside the walls of the cemetery, including sacrificial trenches, with the complex symbolizing the overall layout of the capital. Ongoing archeological work continues to yield more traces of structures and artifacts, including the imperial burial palace, side palaces, gardens and temples. The excavated sites include the bronze cart and horse trench, the western tomb construction site, horse trench, rare bird and animal trench, tombs for the princes and princesses and tomb builders. Each of the sites has enriched our knowledge and understanding of the Qin system, culture, clothing and material civilization.

The Ming Xiaoling Tomb—The Initial Mausoleum of Ming Dynasty

Xiaoling Tomb of the Ming Dynasty, located at the south foot of Mt. Zhong on the south bank of the lower reaches of Yangtze River, in the eastern suburban of Nanjing, Jiangsu Province, is the mausoleum of Zhu Yuanzhang (reign 1368–1398), the founding emperor of the Ming Dynasty.

The mausoleum consists of two major sections. The first section is from the Gateway of dismounting Horse to the Lingxing Gate at the end of Sacred Passage (tomb avenue), of which the approach is 1,800 meters long. Historical records indicate that the mausoleum had a grand red wall, 22.5 kilometers long, enclosing the whole tomb area. Unfortunately, this large group of buildings was ruined by wars and all the wooden structures were destroyed. However, we can still see the exquisite stone carvings from the stone bases and imagine how magnificent it looked like 600 years ago.

Northwards from the Great Golden Gate, a huge roofless

Xiaoling Tomb of the Ming Dynasty in Nanjing.

The stele that read "The Tablet of Deified Exploits and Holy Virtues of the Ming Emperor" in the Square Castle of Ming Dynasty's Xiaoling Tomb.

45

The stone sculptures of civilian official on the Sacred Passage of Ming Dynasty's Xiaoling Tomb.

stone Golden Gate, a huge roofless stone tablet pavilion can be seen; it is the Square Castle, as local people call it. Its top is gone but the surrounding walls and four archways still remain. In the middle of the building, there stands an 8.78 meters stele.

Behind the tablet pavilion (the Square Castle) is the Sacred Passage, which is lined on both sides with 12 pairs of giant stone animals in 6 kinds. For each kind of the animals, there are one pair standing and the other kneeling. The standing pair is working and the kneeling resting and they are on duty alternately. The real purpose of building these animals is to demonstrate the royal magnificence and the emperor's dignity, to drive away evil spirits and guard the tomb. The first two pairs of animals are lions, king of the beasts symbolizing power. The second two pairs of animals are called Bi Xie, a unicorn-shaped mythical animal, said to be clever and capable of distinguishing between good and evil. The following pairs of animals include camels, elephants, kylins or Chinese unicorns and horses.

Regarded as the most important one of all the Ming tombs,

Xiaoling Tomb's burial system served as a link between its past and future in that it inherited the cream of the imperial burial systems of the Han, Tang, and Song Dynasties, added unique innovations to them, and created the imperial burial system used by both the Ming and Qing Emperors. The Tombs of the Ming and Qing Emperors in Beijing, Hubei, Liaoning, and Hebei due to different historical stages were all built in conformity with the scale and style of the Xiaoling Tomb in Nanjing. The Xiaoling Tomb of the Ming Dynasty was a milestone in the history of imperial burial system in ancient China, because Thirteen Tombs of the Ming Emperors, Xiaoling Tomb of the Ming Dynasty, the Eastern Tombs of the Qing Dynasty and the Western Tombs of the Qing Dynasty all inherited the standards of the Xiaoling Tomb. Standardizing the overall layout and genre of over 20 imperial tombs of the Ming and Qing Dynasties over more than 500 years, the Xiaoling Tomb enjoys high position in history with far-reaching influences.

The Ming Tombs in Beijing.

The Ming Tombs—The Best Representative of Mausoleum Group

The Ming tombs lie in a broad valley to the south of Tianshou (Longevity of Heaven) Mountain in Changping County, about 50 kilometers northwest of Beijing proper. To the southwest of this valley, a branch of the Yanshan Range suddenly to breaks

The 7,300-meters-long Sacred Passage of Beijing Ming Tombs. The stone sculptures of animals and human beings include kneeling camels, standing elephants, standing kylins, etc.

Long'en Hall, the major building of Changling Tomb (Emperor Yongle) in Beijing Ming Tombs, is situated on the three-storey marble dado.

off and forms a natural gateway to the 40-quare-kilometer basin in which the tombs were built. This gateway is "defended" on each side by the Dragon and Tiger hills, which are said to protect this sacred area from winds carrying evil influences. Thirteen out of the 16 Ming emperors are buried in this peaceful valley.

Visitors first pass by an elegant, five-arched white marble memorial archway. Built in 1540, this 29-meter-wide and 14-meter-high structure, with its delicate bas-relief carvings of lions, dragons and lotuses, is still in near-perfect condition. About one kilometer to the northeast of this archway stands the Dahong Gate (Great Red Gate), the outermost gate of the entire mortuary complex.

The Great Red Gate marks the beginning of the 7-kilometer-long Shendao (Sacred Passage), which leads to the entrance of the Changling, the tomb of Emperor Yongle (reign 1403–1424). Continuing on, one comes to a tall square stele pavilion, with four tall white Huabiaos (stone ornamental column) set at each of its four corners, standing boldly in the center of the Sacred Passage. The pavilion houses a huge stone tortoise by the famous Avenue of the Animals, where pairs of lions, elephants, camels.

Horses and a number of mythological beasts line the road. There are 24 stone creatures in all. These beasts are followed in turn by a group of 12 stone human figures, which represent the funeral cortege of the deceased emperors. Carved in 1540, this group is made up of military, civil and meritorious officials. Immediately beyond these human figures are the Longfeng Gate (Dragon and Phoenix Gate), which are pierced with three archways.

Compared to the other 12 tombs the Changling is the largest and best preserved. Built on a south-facing slope, the Changling's three courtyards are entirely surrounded by walls. The first courtyard extends from the massive three-arched entrance gate to the Long'en Gate (Gate of Eminent Favor); on the east of this courtyard stands a pavilion, which contains a stone tablet, a stone camel and a stone dragon. Inside the second courtyard stands the Hall of Eminent Favor. The central portion of the stairway, which leads up to this great hall is carved with designs of sea beats and dragons. To the east and west of the hall stand two ritual stoves where bolts of silk and inscribed scrolls were set aflame as offerings to the emperor's ancestors. The dimensions of the Hall of Eminent Favor (67 x 29 meters) closely match the dimensions of the Taihe Hall (Hall of Supreme Harmony) in the Forbidden City, which makes it one of the largest wooden buildings in China. Four giant wooden columns and 28 smaller pillars support this structure, The four large columns are 14.3 meters high and 1.17 meters in diameter, and are extraordinary for the fact that they are each a single trunk of Phoebe nanmu.

Overground buildings of Dingdongling Tomb (Empress Cixi) represent the highest architectural technology among all Qing tombs.

The Eastern and Western Tombs of the Qing Dynasty— The Most Systematic Mausoleum of Emperors, Empresses, and Imperial Concubines

Eastern Tombs of the Qing Dynasty, located in the Malan Vally of Zunhua City, Hebei Province, is one of the imperial mausoleums of the Qing Dynasty. The Tombs were started to be built in the 18th year in the reign of Shunzhi (1661). Altogether 161 members of the imperial family including five emperors and 15 empresses were buried here. The five tombs for Emperors are, namely, Xiaoling Tomb for Emperor Shunzhi, Jingling Tomb

Longfeng Gate (Dragon and Phoenix Gate) of Yuling Tomb (Emperor Qianlong) in the Eastern Tombs of the Qing Dynasty.

for Emperor Kangxi, Yuling Tomb for Emperor Qianlong, Dingling Tomb for Emperor Xianfeng, and Huiling Tomb for Emperor Tongzhi. The four tombs for Empresses are, namely, Zhaoxiling Tomb for Empress Xiaozhuangwen, Xiaodongling Tomb for Empress Xiaohuizhang, Dingdongling Tomb for Empress Ci'an, and Xiaodongling Tomb for Empress Cixi. Eastern Tombs of the Qing Dynasty provide both precious material evidences for studies of burial system, funeral standard, sacrificing etiquettes, and architectural art and technique in the Qing Dynasty as well as typical examples for the studies of politics, economics, military, culture, science, and art at that time.

Western Tombs of the Qing Dynasty, located in the Yi County of Hebei Province, 120 kilometers south-west of Beijing, was built between 1730 and 1915. The Tombs cover an area of 1,842 hectares with a buffer zone of 6,458 hectares, including 14 mausoleums and two ancillary buildings, the Yongfu Temple and the imperial palace. Because it is the latest mausoleum complex ever built in the Qing Dynasty and the last site of tombs of feudal emperors

Western Tombs of the Qing Dynasty.

Stele of Muling Tomb (Emperor Daoguang) in the Western Tombs of the Qing Dynasty.

in China, Western Tombs are the comprehensive expression of Chinese ancient architectural art both in form, technology, and design ideas, and they are also the best-preserved Qing mausoleum. With abundant material evidences and historical documents, Western Tombs illustrate the Chinese mausoleum architectural art and genre and the significant development and changes of the religious believe of the imperial family between 1730s to early 20th century from different aspects.

The Palaces of Gods

Religions in ancient China were formed by three main schools of thoughts: Confucianism, Buddhism, and Taoism. As the saying goes, "Confucianism is the way to peace and prosperity; Buddhism is for the cultivation of the self through meditation, and Taoism is for the cultivation of the body. Other religions that coexisted with these three fundamental sects include Islam, Christianity and Catholicism.

In its earliest stage, Confucianism was only a concept and did not involve gods and sorcery. During the reign of Emperor Wudi (reign 140 BC–87 BC) of Han Dynasty, Confucianism became a government-run school of thought—deemed for the unification of thinking and for the stabilization of the nation. The founder, Kong Qiu (Confucius), was respected as the "Teacher of Eternity", and temples in honor of him spread far and wide across the nation, and they could be found in many cities and provinces. Confucius temples can also be regarded as a form of religious architecture. Other than Confucius temples, academies for classical learning were also considered by as a form of Confucius architecture.

In 5th Century BC, Gautama Siddhartha founded Buddhism in ancient India. And as early as the later period of the Western Han Dynasty (202 BC–8 BC), Buddhism was brought into China—among the commercial and cultural exchanges—via the Silk Road. In the Eastern Han Dynasty, Buddhism began to merge with the indigenous cultures of China, resulting in a Buddhism that is rich in Chinese features and which became one of the mainstreams of China's traditional thinking. Buddhist monasteries, Buddhist pagodas and Buddhist Grottos soon became a significant representation of China's ancient architecture.

Taoism is an indigenous religion of China which studies how human beings exist in the world, and how they build their relationships with nature and society, as well as how they can live healthily and obtain longevity and immortality.

Islam first spread into China in the mid-7th Century. In its process of transmission and development, it assimilated elements of traditional Chinese culture. It adopted Confucius thinking in explaining Islamic doctrine and gradually, the unique China's Islamic faith took shape. The mosques found in other places across the country are just as diverse in styles, with several of these mosques adopting the model of the Chinese courtyard house.

During the Tang Dynasty in the year 635, the Nestorian sect of Christianity was spread into China, but soon went into decline. During the period of Yuan, the Nestorian sect once again spread into China, along with the Roman Catholics. But it went into decline and almost vanished as the Yuan Dynasty was destroyed. During the Ming and Qing dynasties, especially after the Opium War, the different Christian sects came in succession into China to spread the Christian faith, at a scale that way surpassed their predecessors'. The missionaries from different Christians sects went far and wide, and into the remotest parts of China in their common quest. They left an ever-lasting impact on China's society, along with the many churches they built.

Confucian Architecture

Confucius Temple

During the period of Spring and Autumn, the great thinker and educator Kongzi (Confucius) integrated the schools of thought and literature of the kingdoms of Lu, Zhou, Song and Qi, and compiled the *Five Classics* and the *Book of Rites*. He advocated the idea of governing the country based on rites and propriety, and further developed a system of rites and founded the academy of Confucian learning.

Over a period of 2,000 years, Confucianism gradually became an orthodox culture of China and has a great impact on countries in East Asia and Southeast Asia— becoming a foundation of Oriental cultural. In order to consolidate power, a majority of China's rulers adopted Confucianism as a form of control over their subjects and showed great reverence to Confucius as a divine character.

In the second year following the passing of Confucius, the king of Lu converted Confucius' former residence in Qufu of Shandong as a temple as a commemoration to

The panorama of Confucian Temple in Qufu, Shandong.

the great thinker. In 195 BC, the founder of Han Dynasty, Liu Bang, held a grand sacrificial ceremony to offer sacrifices to Confucius. As more honorific titles were conferred on Confucius, the scale of Qufu Confucius Temple began to increase in size. From the Eastern Han Dynasty to the Qing Dynasty, it went through 15 major and numerous minor renovations to become a huge cluster of temple buildings. Its scale and styles were comparable to the imperial temples and became a unique example of altar temples.

Qufu Confucius Temple is comprised of three compounds—the temple, the residence and the tomb. The Confucius' Residence was the residential compound of the offspring of Confucius and is the largest residence in China aside from the palaces of the Ming and Qing emperors. The Confucius Tomb is located to the north of Qufu and it is the cemetery of Confucius and his family.

The scale of today's Confucius Temple took its shape in the Qing Dynasty during the reign of Emperor Yongzheng. The plane of the temple is long and narrow, measuring 600 meters in the north-south direction. The width of the temple measures 140 meters. There are altogether nine courtyards in the temple, with the north-south

The Lingxing Gate of Qufu Confucian Temple.

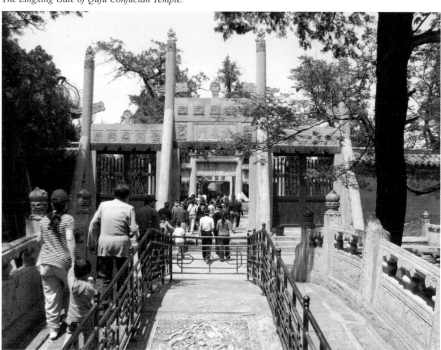

The Dacheng Hall of Qufu Confucian Temple.

axis as its center. There are about 400 over halls, altars and chambers, 54 gateways and 13 imperial tablet-pavilions within the temple grounds.

The first three courtyards in the temple are meant for directional purpose. In front of the entrance is a screen wall commemorating Confucius for his impeccable character and his wisdoms. Upon passing the first three courtyards of different sizes, one would reach Kuiwen Chamber, which is the library of Confucius Temple.

The stone columns engraved with patterns of twisting dragons before the Dacheng Hall of Qufu Confucian Temple.

Behind Kuiwen Court are 13 pavilions—each houses an imperial stone tablet. Then one would reach Dacheng Gate. Within the square of Dacheng Gate is a rectangular pavilion called Apricot Altar, and it was the former address of Confucius' lecture hall.

After passing Apricot Altar, one would reach the main building of Confucius Temple—Dacheng Hall, Qin Hall and Shengji Hall. Dacheng Hall is meant for holding grand sacrificial ceremonies. Qin Hall is where the altar of Confucius is consecrated. In Shengji Hall, a series of 120 paintings relating the life story of Confucius is displayed.

During the early period of the Tang Dynasty, a system of standards and requirements for building Confucius temples was put in place. Since then, different parts of China began to see the construction of Confucius temples. As Confucianism claimed a

Nanjing Confucius Temple.

dominant position in society and for in recognition of Confucius' contribution in education, all the academies in the country were required to have a Confucius temple built in the compound. The Confucius temples were then functioning as a venue for practicing rites and propriety and paying respect to Confucius.

Confucius temples in the localities were all modeled on the architectural style of Qufu Confucius Temple. The typical layout of the temple would have the prayer hall on the left and the academy on the right. All the features in Qufu Confucius Temple were replicated, which included the screen wall, the gateways and the platform, etc. The only difference is the scale of these structures.

As the deification of Confucius progressed through history, activities that were held in honor of Confucius continued to escalate, to the extent that the Confucius temples surpassed the academies in importance. Instead, the school became an auxiliary building of the temple. Qufu Confucius Temple and other Confucius temples in the country are credited for spreading Confucian learning to the neighboring countries, such as Japan, which had a number of Confucius temples built in the major cities.

Architecture of Academies of Classical Learning

The earliest academy of classical learning first came into being in the middle of Tang Dynasty. It was started by the society using funds they gathered. Founded on official and traditional private learning systems, the academy had its own lectures, collection of books and rites—making up for the inadequacies of official learning.

The dominant role of Confucius learning had long been established in ancient China, whereas the dissemination of Buddhist and Taoist teachings was much broader and therefore, had a deeper impact in society. On top of this, both religions were valued and exploited by the rulers for political purposes. Confucius learning thus became the main school of thought in intellectual learning, while Buddhist and Taoist teachings took on the role of supplementary learning. This became a typical feature in the traditional culture of China.

During the process where Confucianism, Buddhism and Taoism were vying for dominance, Confucianism assimilated Buddhist teaching to substantiate its philosophy theories—giving birth to Neo-Confucianism. This resulted in much constructive interaction between the different schools of thought. The academy was just fitting for such a function.

The main gate of Yuelu Academy in Changsha, Hunan.

59

The development process of academies during the Ming Dynasty was marked by many ups and downs. Scholars such as Wang Yangming and Zhan Ruoshui worked actively to develop the academies, leading them to a period of prosperity. Along with other schools of thought popular during that time, they actively took part in political debates—forging an important place in the history of China.

The academies finally went into decline during the end of the Qing Dynasty. Finally, it was undertaken by the official authorities and became the predecessors of present-day schools. This marked the end of the academies of classical learning.

The academies of classical learning were gathering place for scholars and literati and were started by leading scholars of the time. They reflected the thinking, lifestyles and aesthetic tastes of the ancient Chinese intellectuals. The traditional thinking of "heaven and man as an entity"—the harmonious relationship between man and nature—was the highest state of being that they aspired to achieve. In selecting an appropriate for the locations for the academies, emphasis was giving to the natural environment that they would be set it. The environment must also allow for variations to be made in the entire building structure so as to enable extensions to be made. And due to the fact that Neo-Confucianism also take into consideration Buddhist teachings, which emphasizes on cultivation of the self and to dissociate oneself from the material world, the academies were frequently built in a tranquil natural scenic spot.

As rites and propriety played an important part in the academies, they were restricted by many traditional systems and thinking. The concept of symmetrical layout and the central axis along which the main buildings were built were crucial factors to be considered. Within the academy's compound were courtyards, gardens, corridors and spacious halls. The buildings were also constructed in accordance with the terrain, reflecting the harmony between man and nature. The lecture halls, which numbered three to five, were the main buildings along the central axis. In front of the lecture halls were special courtyards, which helped in giving prominence to the status of the main buildings in the academy and allowed space for further extensions.

The garden of Yuelu Academy.

The library of Yuelu Academy.

The library was another important building in the academy and it usually occupied about two or three levels. It was usually located at the back of the academy, set in a tranquil environment. The ancestral temple or the main hall was for the consecration of the teachers and deans. Certain academies also include a Confucius temple as part of it. Other than these main buildings, the academy had also a small courtyard house that was the dean's residence, as well as hostels for the students. The academy was also surrounded by landscaped gardens. Subsequently, when official authorities took over the operations of the academies, other buildings such as supervision halls, military lecture halls, archery galleries, and examination halls were added to the compounds.

Ancient Chinese intellectuals were against the idea of extravagance in building structures. Instead, they advocated simplicity in the architecture of the academies. The academies assimilated various architecture styles of the localities and pursued the ideal of natural beauty. The buildings must be

61

functional and meet the everyday needs of the people. Because of this, the academies were simple and humble buildings with minimal decorative elements. They contrasted sharply with the imperial architecture styles. A profound cultural intension was the unique feature of the academies.

Buddhist Architecture

During the 2nd century BC, Emperor Wudi of Han Dynasty sent Zhang Qian on a mission to explore the western region, or Central Asia. With this quest, the Silk Road, which connected East Asian and West Asia, was established. Around AD, Buddhism, which originated in India, was spread into China via the Silk Road. Not only that Buddhism was welcomed by the masses, it also won the hearts and support of the political rulers. During the period of Wei, Jin and the Southern and Northern Dynasties (220–581), the spread of Buddhism was at its peak—to the extent that it was regarded by Emperor Wudi of Liang Dynasty (reign 502–549) as the national religion. It was at this stage that the building of Buddhist temples reached great heights. This trend was even reflected in many literary works of the time. The Tang Dynasty

Figures of Buddha in Yungang Grotto in Datong of Shanxi.

The beautiful scene of Mt. E'mei.

was the flourishing period of Buddhism. Not only that China's Buddhism was further developed within the country, it was also brought to Korea, Japan and Vietnam. The Yuan Dynasty rulers were fervent supporters of Tibetan Buddhism. Hence, many Tibetan Buddhist temples were built during that period.

Today, Buddhism that is popular among the Han Chinese people is known as Han Buddhism, where as Buddhism that spread into Tibet from India and Nepal is known as Tibetan Buddhism. Commonly known as Lama Sect, it is predominant in Tibet, Gansu, Qinghai and Inner Mongolia, with Lhasa and ShiGaTse as centers of the religion. In Yunnan's Xishuangbanna, there are traces of Hinayana Buddhism, and the architecture style adopted in this region is unlike those Buddhist temples that are found in the Han Chinese regions.

There is a Chinese saying: "All the famous mountains under the sky are populated with monks". This probably came from the fact that in order to study the dharma and meditate, a tranquil spot is a prerequisite. Hence, most of the Buddhist temples and monasteries are built in the mountains. The temples can be built at any part of the mountain, be it the foot of the mountain, on the mountainside or right on its peak. It can also be built near a mountain, across a river, or blended in with the natural environment. The monks also created names of religious significance and attached them to scenic spots. These mountains gained popularity because of the Buddhist

The first Buddhist temple of China—Baima Temple (White Horst Temple) in Luoyang, Henan.

temples built in them, and the temples flourished because of the popularity of the mountains. The four mountains in China that had gained their fame from the Buddhist temples built in them are Mt. Wutai in Shanxi, Mt. E'mei in Sichuan, Mt. Putuo in Zhejiang and Mt. Jiuhua in Anhui.

In ancient China, the sovereign of a ruler was regarded to be higher than the power of God. As the Buddhist flourished and the number of temples escalated, the privileges given to the monks and nuns began to take on greater significance, which threatened the authority of the imperial court. Emperor Taiwudi (reign 423–452) of Northern Wei Dynasty, Emperor Wudi (reign 560–578) of Northern Zhou Dynasty, Emperor Wuzong (reign 841–846) of Tang Dynasty all had a role in stamping out the power and influence of the Buddhist monks, causing much bloodshed. However, such large-scale incidents took up only a small fraction in China's history. Subsequently, Buddhism continued to develop in China for almost 2,000 years. As such, Buddhist architecture became a feature of China's major architectures. The most commonly seen would be the Buddhist temples, pagodas, and grottos.

Buddhist Temples

Buddhist temple is a major type in China's religious buildings. It is for the consecration of the Buddha's image, the holding of Buddhist rites, and where the monks reside.

Legend has it that in the 7th year of the Eastern Han Dynasty (64 AD), Emperor Mingdi dreamt of an imposing golden man. His minister Fu Yi told him that there was a god in the west and his name is Buddha. Hence, Emperor Mingdi dispatched the officials Cai Yin and Qin Jing to seek for Buddhist teaching in India. The party returned to the city of Luoyang with two high monks, Kasyapa-matanga and Dharmaraksa, along with Buddhist scriptures and the image of Buddha. The hosts arranged for the high monks to stay at Honglu Temple, which at the time, was meant for receiving foreign guests. The following year, the monks had their own residence built, and it was named Baima Temple (White Horse Temple), owing to the fact that they arrived into on white horses. Baima Temple thus became the first Buddhist temple ever being built in China.

As Buddhism developed rapidly in China, it faced a shortage of Buddhist temples. In aid of this problem, many court officials and rich merchants offered their own residence to function as temples. These were known as "residence temples", and its front hall was used as the temple hall and the back used as the lecture hall. One of the main characteristics of Buddhism is to attach the least significance to the material world and focus on the spiritual. The traditional courtyard house, which fits in with this concept, soon became a definitive architectural model of a Buddhist temple.

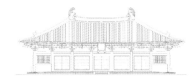

The elevation of the main hall of Foguang Temple in Mt. Wutai, Shanxi.

Hanging Temple in Datong, Shanxi.

65

In the initial stage, Buddhist temples in China were modeled against the ones in India, that is, the pagoda as the center of the building, or with the pagoda in the front and the hall in the back. As Buddhist temples took on an indigenous, Chinese design, the pagoda was being placed in the back of the temple, while the hall became the center of the entire temple. The two oldest, still existing wooden buildings in China are both Buddhist temples. They are Shanxi's Nanchan Temple main hall and Fuoguang Temple main hall—both in Mt. Wutai. Their corbel brackets are gigantic, the eaves are deep, and the roofing is smooth and gentle, with succinct decorative elements—a classic Tang Dynasty architecture style.

Once the architecture style of Buddhist temples in China had taken on a definitive shape, one could see that in essence, they had inherited all the original elements in Chinese architecture. A typical Buddhist temple is symmetrically laid out and all the buildings in the temple such as the bell and drum tower, the main hall, and the sutra library are all situated along the axis, while the living quarters for the monks are located at the sides. A very good example of such a temple would be Longxing Temple in Zhengding of Hebei Province. It is the only Song Dynasty temple that is so well preserved and it houses a 24-meter tall image of the "thousand-handed Kwan-yin." Even though the axis of the temple is long, the variety in sizes and designs of all the buildings and the creative use of space within the temple compound give it a refreshing touch.

In Hunyuan of Shanxi Province, there is the Hanging Temple, built during the later period of the Northern Wei Dynasty. It constitutes a group of Buddhist temples that are suspended from the precipitous cliffs of Mt. Heng. The weights of these temples rely entirely on the wooden poles fixed into holes that were chiseled into the cliff. The different halls are then connected with wooden planks. They resemble mansions in the air and are an amazing sight to behold. The Hanging Temples are primarily for the consecration of Buddha, but at the same time, they are influenced by the two other religions—Confucianism and Taoism. The temples are concrete representations of the

The weight of Hanging Temple's building is sustained by the wooden poles inserted into the cliff.

*Potala Palace in Lhasa,
Tibet.*

harmonious relationship between the three major ancient
religions of China.

Tibetan Buddhism (the Lama Sect) advocates the practice of
combining politics and religion, and emphasizes the importance
of religious rites. All the different Buddhist festivals are grand
events to the Tibetans and the scale of the celebrations is
frequently large. The Tibetan Buddhist monasteries are built close
to the mountains, and totally blend in with the natural highland
landscapes. In terms of architecture, the buildings combine the
use of wooden framework of the Chinese people with the local's
stone fortress. The Tibetans also absorbed the decorative styles
of the temples in Nepal to create a stable, grand, and colorful
architectural style. The most representative of this would be the
Potala Palace in Lhasa, Tibet.

Potala Palace was built in the 7th century AD when the Tang
Dynasty's Princess Wencheng married Songtsen Gampo—king
of the Tubo kingdom of Tibet. The palace was specially built to
greet the arrival of Princess Wencheng in Lhasa. The palace was
later incorporated into later buildings to form the present-day
Potala Palace. This process of incorporating other buildings took
many years to complete and took up almost the entire mountain.
The palace is now comprised of the White Palace, the Red Palace,
the "snow" at the foothill and the Dragon King Pool. The White
Palace is where the Dalai Lama resides; it is also a monastery
and for secular use. The Red Palace is meant for religious studies

Different styles of pagodas in China.

and Buddhist prayers. It contains different chapels or halls and houses the relics of the former Dalai Lamas.

In Chengde of Hebei Province where the Summer Palace is located, there are eight Tibetan temples. It is commonly known as Outer Eight Temples. They were built by the Qing rulers for the purpose of uniting the minority ethnic groups—particularly the Buddhists in the Tibetan and Mongolian regions. Among these temples is a replica of Potala Palace.

The Buddhist temples of Yunnan's Dai people and other minority ethnic groups are directly under the influence of Burmese and Thai architectural styles. At the same time, they combined the flexibility of local architecture to create a lively, unrestrained architectural style. The roofs of the buildings are layered and divided into section—enabling it to give prominence to the center of the house. The ridges of the roofs are also decorated with an assortment of ornaments.

Pagodas

Pagodas are ancient Buddhist buildings that are used to house the bone relics of Buddhas and other high monks. In Sanskrit, it is called the "stupa". It is a symbol of the Buddha where the worshippers held in reverence.

Pagoda was brought into China along with Buddhism itself. The stupa of India quickly blended in with the Chinese pagodas to become a unique Chinese-style stupa. There is a pavilion at the base of the stupa to give prominence to the venerated status of the stupa, which was house in the topmost part of the pagoda. The pagoda also has an underground chamber to house treasures such as relics, sutras and images of the Buddha. From such pavilion-style pagodas, other designs of pagodas were created. Even the Lama pagodas and Yunnan's Burmese-style pagodas had been influenced by Chinese elements.

Pagoda group in Shaolin Temple, Henan.

The earliest pagodas were mainly constructed on wooden structures, but they were not durable. During the Southern and Northern Dynasties, people started to build brick pagodas, and by the Tang and Song dynasties, copper and steel pagodas were built. After the Song Dynasty, there were even glazed-tile pagodas and porcelain pagodas. The several thousand still-existing ancient pagodas in China are mainly brick pagodas. The oldest ancient wooden pagoda would be Fogong Temple in Ying County of Shanxi Province. It is so sturdy that it has stood its ground for thousands of year, even after withstanding several major earthquakes.

From a single pagoda, it soon developed to have up to several pagodas built close to one another. In the Shaolin Temple in Henan, there are 220 brick pagodas that were built over thousands of years beginning from the Tang Dynasty till the Qing Dynasty. They came in various designs and boast excellent craftsmanship.

Gradually, the pagodas in China took on practical values, and this was especially so for scholars and men of letters. As a

The wooden pagoda in Ying County at Shanxi, built in 1056.

The stone pagoda in Linggu Temple at Nanjing, built in 1931.

69

Three Pagodas of Chongsheng Temple in Dali, Yunnan.

tall building, one could ascend a pagoda to take in the distant views. With this function in place, there soon emerged many sightseeing tours involving visits to the pagodas. Many Tang Dynasty poets enjoyed moments at the top of the pagodas for poetry recitation and writing sessions, which very quickly became a trend of the time.

With the development of sightseeing at pagodas, the pagodas soon took on military functions and were used in navigation. Very often, such pagodas were built on the pretext of housing Buddhist relics, while its actual purpose was for reconnaissance. The tallest ancient pagoda in China—Liaodi Pagoda, in Hebei— standing at 84 meters was used for such purposes. Some pagodas were used as lighthouses, such as Liuhe Pagoda in Hangzhou.

Other than this, there are many pagodas that are scenic spots that are loved by many visitors, such as the White Pagoda on Qionghua Isle of Beijing's Beihai Park. In Yunnan's Chongsheng Temple are three pagodas that are set in the beautiful Cang Mountain. And Leifeng Pagoda in Hangzhou's West Lake is famous for its depiction in the Chinese classic tale *Madam White Snake*, and welcome many visitors everyday.

In the later period of the 7ᵗʰ century AD, a new form of Buddhist building came into being. They were the monumental Buddhist columns. It is octagonal in shape and on the stone column are inscriptions of sutras. They were used for the commemoration of Buddhist teachings. At a temple that consecrates the image of Buddha, only one such column would be built. As for a temple that consecrates the Bodhisattvas, two to four such monumental columns would be built. The best specimen of monumental columns would be the one built during the Northern Song Dynasty, located in Hebei's Zhao County, and it is known for its excellent craftsmanship in stone carving.

Grottos

China's grottos had their originations in India's grotto temples, and this model was spread into China sometime during the period of the Southern and Northern Dynasties. It blended in rapidly with Chinese traditional elements and left behind a huge number of grottos. The development of grottos reached its peak during the periods of Wei, Jin and Tang

Yungang Grotto in Datong of Shanxi.

71

The 13.25-meters-high figure of Puxian Bodhisattva in Longmen Grotto in Luoyang, Henan.

dynasties. The earliest grottos were predominantly spread along the route that connects China and India—The Silk Road.

Not only that these grottos recorded the history of Buddhism in China, but the frescoes in the grottos are also a reflection of ancient China's development in art and culture. China's most popular grottos are Mogao Grotto in Dunhuang of Gansu, Yungang Grotto in Datong of Shanxi, and Longmen Grotto in Luoyang of Henan. Other well-known grottos include Sichuan's Dazu Grotto, Gansu's Tianshui Maijishan Grotto, and Shanxi's Taiyuan Tianlongshan Grotto, and Gansu's Yongjing Bingling Temple Grotto. Out of all these grottos, Mogao Grotto is the largest in size. The process of development is also the longest and is broadest in content, and the most well preserved.

Cave No.20 of Yungang Grotto in Datong, Shanxi. The figure of Buddha is 13.75 meters in height and is the classic work of Yungang Grotto.

Dunhuang of Gansu Province is situated at the junction of the north and south sections of the Silk Road. Once, it was a bustling city that saw a high volume of trade, and it was populated with Buddhist temples. Mogao Grotto is commonly known as the "Thousand Buddha Cave". From the period of the Sixteen Kingdoms (304–439) till the Yuan Dynasty, Mogao Grotto went through a development process that spanned more than ten dynasties. Today, the cliffs of Dunhuang are full of grottos, all interconnected with wooden planks. Within the grottos are beautiful frescos and painted sculptures.

Mogao Grotto was built in the architecture style that was common during the period of the Tang and Song dynasties. These eaves of the grottos employed the use of techniques that were common in China for building wooden structures, reflecting the process of assimilation of Chinese culture. In the frescoes that were created in different dynasties, what one see are the scenes of daily social activities of the ancient people. The characters of the frescoes present a good study on the costumes and accessories worn by the different ethnic groups in different periods.

Mogao Grotto in Dunhuang, Gansu.

The Buddha images back then were strongly influenced by the Central Asian art. The looks of the characters and their costumes are rich in Indian and Persian flavors. It was until the Northern Wei Dynasty that the depiction of the characters in the frescoes started to change. One noticeable change would be the

73

"Flying Apsaras" in Mogao Grotto.

Leshan Buddha in Sichuan.

costumes, which had become more Chinese in style. The Tang Dynasty was the peak of the development of Buddhist art. During this time, the images of Buddha became plumper and more lifelike, and the decorative lines in the images took on very obvious changes as well. The palaces and the various buildings such as pavilion, chambers, pagodas and bridges depicted in the frescoes during this time became treasures to historians in leading them to new historical finds around the whole of China.

Worth mentioning here is one of the famous frescoes of Dunhuang called the "Flying Apsaras". Asparas is a female mythical spirit, which, in Buddhism, has a flair in music and the dance of flight. Though it does not carry a pair of wings, the ancient Chinese artists liked to depict her in a dance of flight, like she is flying into the sky. It is a mesmerizing character in Dunhuang's frescos that have stole the hearts of many visitors.

As the images of Buddha built at the grottos were built increasingly larger, the development of grotto art began to be shifted to the exterior of the caves. During the Tang Dynasty, the largest image of Buddha in China—Leshan Buddha in Sichuan—came into being. This huge image of Buddha was carved out of a cliff, in accordance to the original height of the cliff. The construction of the image began in the Tang Dynasty in 713, and took a total of 90 years to complete. The Buddha image measures 71 meters in height, 24 meters in width. The ears of the images measure 7 meters in length, and can seat two people within each ear. The foot of the image can hold more than a hundred people. One can barely imagine its actual size. To date, Leshan Buddha is the world's largest Buddha image.

Taoist Architecture

Taoism is China's indigenous religion that has its roots in folk sorcery and mysticism that first came into being during the Shang Dynasty. It involves alchemy, philosophy and various forms of sorcery. It was not until the Eastern Han Dynasty when Master Zhang Daoling developed a school of thought known as the "Way of Wudou" that Taoism was established as a religion comprising based on the teachings of the founder of Taoism—Laozi, who also wrote *Tao Te Ching*.

As Taoism originated from the common people, the earliest venues for religious activities were in the mountain regions. Hence, the primary Taoist buildings at that time were caves and an assortment of residences in the mountains and rural areas.

Temple of City Gods in Shanghai

75

The choice of environment for the practice of the religion was not very stringent in terms of its requirement. All that was necessary was to be away in seclusion.

During the period of Wei and Jin dynasties, Taoism borrowed extensively from Confucianism and Buddhism in order to fulfill the criteria set by the feudal rulers. This means that there must be a system of rites and rituals in place in order for it to function as a religion. Hence, a new concept was derived from it. It advocated that all Taoist must fundamentally be loyal, filial and compassionate. They were to attempt looking for a formula in making pills and concoction in order to obtain immortality. Hence Taoism was actually a manifestation of the rulers' desire to rule over the spiritual aspect of the people, and it was welcome by them. From then on, Taoism began its development from the rural regions to the towns and cities in order to merge with the imperial authority. The proper nouns used in describing imperial buildings were soon used to denote Taoist buildings as well.

Beginning from the Tang Dynasty, Taoism enjoyed a period of supremacy and was comparable with Buddhism. It was highly revered in the Song Dynasty and all the ancestral temples at the time were regarded as Taoist temples. At the beginning of the Yuan Dynasty, the Taoist master Qiu Chuji met with Genghi Khan and obtained his support, thereupon pushing Taoism to great heights and it was then that Taoist temples were built across the country. It was during the Ming and Qing dynasties that Taoism went into decline.

For over 2000 years, the Taoist temples were mainly built in the mountains, which was a practice similar to the Buddhists. But they were actually very different in essence.

In the first place, Taoism teaches the role of nature and the relationship between human beings and the natural elements. Hence, Taoist buildings must be located in a natural environment as well. They must also be in harmony with nature and their environments. When selecting an appropriate location for the temples, the concepts of the yin and yang and the Eight Trigrams must be at play. In selecting an appropriate location amidst a natural environment, the Taoists believe that a harmonious

Zixiao Taoist Temple at Mt. Wudang, Hubei.

The snow landscape of Bixia Taoist Temple at Mt. Tai, Shandong.

relationship can be struck when science, art and nature merge as one, and hence attaining immortality became a possibility.

Secondly, in order for the Taoist priests to attain immortality, they have to be close to heaven, or a place that is out of this world. In legends, these places were usually found in the seas, mountains and caves. Hence, building a temple in the mountains allowed the Taoist priests to be closer to these unworldly places.

Thirdly, in order to study and conduct experiments to find a formula to obtaining a pill that would bring about immortality, the Taoist believed that a tranquil environment that is free of distractions would be just right for the cause. In Taoism, this is a sacred practice and not to be violated. This concept also affects the choice of location and the layout of the Taoist temples.

For purpose of good *feng shui*, some of the Taoist temples were built high up on the peaks of famous mountains. Some examples of such temples would be Mt. Wudang in Hubei, Mt. Qingcheng in Sichuan, and Mt. Lao in Shandong. Perched on

Shangqing Taoist Temple at Mt. Qingcheng, Sichuan.

the top of these mountains, the Taoist temples are regarded as imposing towers.

Once Taoism became an official religion, the Taoist priests no longer practiced the Way in caves or huts but in beautiful, comfortable temples. However, the building materials were all taken from the local areas and they were neither extravagant nor luxurious. And the designs of the temples generally retained the rustic and simple characteristics of a common residence.

Taoism is a multi-divinity religion that combines the wisdoms of Confucius, Buddha and Laozi. This was also applied in the designs of Taoist temples. As the different sects in Taoism could cause confusions to the masses, in order to facilitate the spread of the religion, Taoism borrowed the idea from the "Three Embodiments of Buddha" and formed its very own "Taoist Trinity". This trinity was comprised of the most divine gods in the religion. Hence, in Taoist temples, the Trinity Halls are the most important and prominent buildings in the compounds. The Taoist also incorporated the teachings of Confucius in the area of rites and propriety and applied this concept to the gods as well. The buildings that consecrated the gods of different levels thus influenced the overall layout of a Taoist temple.

The main hall of the Taoist temple is a classic imperial building. The Taoists primarily consecrate their founder Laozi, whose altar is placed in the center of the Trinity Hall. The Trinity Hall and the halls that consecrate other god of high status are all placed along the central axis of the temple.

Presently, all the existing Taoist temples are dated back to the Ming and the Qing dynasties. Yongle Palace is China's earliest Taoist temple. It houses 28 lively statues that date back to the Yuan Dynasty and are exquisitely crafted clay sculptures. Other well-known Taoist temples can be found at Hubei's Mt. Wudang Sichuan's Mt. Qingcheng—which are now parts of UNESCO World Cultural Heritage.

Erwang Shrine at Mt. Qingcheng, Sichuan.

Islamic Architecture

Following the flow of the Islamic faith into China in the middle of 7th Century AD, many mosques were built by the various ethnic Muslim minorities—for the purpose of practicing the Islamic faith. Islam has been long embedded in China's society. Hence the Islamic architecture has its own unique style, which sets themselves apart from the Islamic architecture in the Middle Eastern countries. They are mainly a blend between China's local and ethnic architecture styles.

The place of worship for the Muslim is called a "mosque". It is built facing the direction of the Mecca, the sacred land of the Muslims. There is a lot of freedom given to the choice of the mosque's location, and it is not restricted by whether it should be in the city or the countryside. At the same time, as the Muslims are very particular about purity, the choice of location where a mosque is to built has to be a place where it is clean and dry.

There are two types of Islamic buildings in China. The first includes the mosques and the tombs of the imams (Islamic religious leader) and they can be found all across the country in different inland provinces. Basically, they are Han Chinese buildings with alterations added for carrying out Islamic activities. The other type refers to the mosques and the Geys' Mazars—tomb of an ancient Islamic sage—prevalent in Xinjiang Uygur Autonomous Region. For this latter type of Islamic buildings, they are much closer to traditional cultures of Central Asia and embody more unique characteristics in their architect and decorative styles.

Mosques in China's Hinterland

The Islamic faith was brought into China during the Tang Dynasty. At that time a sea route was developed for trading, and it was called the "Maritime Silk Road". The Arab merchants, who were Muslims, became the pioneers of China's Islamic faith. They came via the sea and left behind a legacy of Islamic art in the mosques that they built.

In the early period, the mosques built in the hinterland were directly influenced by the architectural style of Central Asia, such as Shenyou Mosque in Fujian's Quanzhou. The dome of the mosque was constructed aventurine, the prayer hall was laid out crosswise, the windows are simple and undecorated, and a *mihrab* with Arabic scripts engraved on it—all are similar to Central Asia's architecture.

The Great Mosque of Hetian, Xinjiang.

With the assimilation of Han culture, China's mosque began to make use of the techniques, materials, carpentry and traditional layout of Han architecture to create a uniquely Chinese Islamic architecture, in accordance with Islamic teaching. It became a norm then that a mosque would inhabit traits of Arabian architecture styles and Chinese architecture elements. For instance, the domes and tipped roofs are of Arabian influence, where as the hexagonal and octagonal tile roofs are of Chinese influence.

The roof of Fenghuang Temple (Phoenix Temple) in Hangzhou displays a blend of traditional Chinese architectural style and Islamic architectural style.

To a certain degree, the traditional religious buildings of the Han Chinese such as the Taoist temples are variations of the common residence, built against the layout of a courtyard house. Such buildings emphasize a symmetrical layout, and the components such as wooden beams, tiled roofs, and elaborately carved beams. These features are seen in the mosques built in the later period. The mosque is a place of worship for the Muslims and it is not a place where they consecrate their god. The only difference that is found in the mosques and traditional courtyard houses is the direction that they face. For the mosques, it has to be facing the direction of Mecca in the west, where as the courtyard house is laid out on a north-south axis. Huajuexiang Mosque in Xi'an is a typical example of a courtyard-type mosque.

The main prayer hall of the mosque is where prayers are held and it usually covers a wide area to accommodate the people. It also occupies the most prominent spot in the mosque. One important feature in the mosque is the *qibla*. The *qibla* indicates the direction of Mecca and it is actually the niche—called a *mihrab*—that is fixed into a wall. The *qibla* is the most

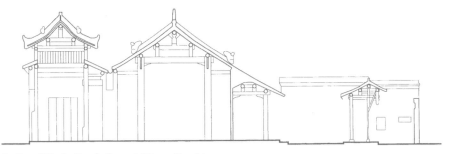

Section of Xianhe Temple (Immortal Crane Temple).

The mihrab *and* mimbar *in the main hall of Beijing Niujie Mosque.*

important part of the mosque and it is usually constructed as a small ornamental shrine-like structure in the wall. The prayer hall has also a pulpit with ten steps, symbolizing the seat where Prophet Mohammed lectured. The imam, or Islamic leader, is only allowed to the third flight of steps—called the *mimbar.*

At the front of the prayer hall is a corridor where the worshippers leave their shoes. Islam does not advocate idol worship. During prayers, the worshipper would face the west in the direction of Mecca. Hence the form of the plane allows much freedom and variety in design. And in order to accommodate a large congregation, the prayer hall would usually link a few building towards the direction of Mecca. For such building structure, each hall would have its own roof, instead of having one huge one for all the buildings as a whole. The sight of such a mosque resembles a mountain range. It is also a unique architecture style for China's mosques.

The minaret—known as light tower in China—in the mosque is for the purpose of calling the Muslims for prayers. The minaret of Huaisheng Mosque in Guangzhou has a unique design. Called the Light Minaret, it is a cylindrical brick structure that measures 36.3 meters in height. It has a central pillar with a winding staircase leading to the top. At the top is a platform with balustrades from which prayer calls are made, and rising from the platform is a column with a pavilion at its top. Because of this special minaret, Huaisheng Mosque is also known as Lighthouse Mosque.

According to Islam, all Muslims are to go through a period of fasting during the ninth month of the Islamic lunar calendar. This is known as Ramadan and during the whole of this month, Muslims are to fast between sunrise and sunset. As this period of fasting is based on the phase of the moon, hence, an observatory is built at a high point in the mosque. In the middle of the Ming Dynasty, the Muslim educator Hu Dengzhou (1552–1597) of Shaanxi returned from pilgrimage in Mecca, and began a series of lectures in the mosque. This was how a building meant for conducting lectures in the mosque first came into being and spread to other parts of the country.

The Islamic faith emphasizes on the importance of keeping

The light tower of Huaisheng Temple in Guangzhou.

The light tower of International Bazaar in Urumqi.

oneself clean as a symbol of one's purity. Before prayers, the Muslims are to clean and wash themselves. Hence a pool for washing and a washing area are indispensable in a mosque.

The colors used in the mosques are primarily cold colors such as blue, green, white and black. This choice of colors has to do with the dry and hot weather conditions of the Arab regions, and it is also in keeping with the Islamic teaching of purity. The mosques in China are also influenced by this choice of colors, hence the green bricks, grey tiles and blue glazed tiles for the roofs. It was only when the emperor had given a title to the mosque could colors such as yellow be used for the glazed tiles. Even then, it would be matched with a green outline so as not to appear too showy.

Decorative ornaments constitute an important element in Islam architecture. However, unlike a typical mosque that uses mosaic and cement as construction materials for ornaments, the mosques in China used wood and bricks, on which decorative designs were carved and painted. However, only patterns of plants can be used and patterns of animals are strictly prohibited. Due to the influence of Han culture, carvings of patterns also appeared on tiles used in the mosques.

The mosques in China do share similarities in the decorative aspect with the mosques in the Arab world. This is seen in the Quran verses that adorned the walls in the calligraphic form for decorative purposes, which is seldom seen in other forms of building art. In China's mosques, one can even find the combination of Chinese and Arabic calligraphy in inscribed boards, which are only common in Chinese culture.

The focal point of decoration in the prayer hall of a mosque is the *mihrab*, which is usually inscribed with verses from the Quran, or have simple patterns carved on it. It catches the attention of the people, yet retains the respect and elegance. The mosque in Niujie Street of Beijing has a *mihrab* that is exquisitely crafted—which is likely due to the fact that Beijing was once the imperial city. It even employs the use of the color red and gold and exudes a rich aesthetic beauty. It can be considered the grandest mosque in the country.

Another Islamic architecture that is worth mentioning is the tomb, which is designed in the shape of an Eight Trigrams, with three eaves on the roof. This is a variation in design that was exclusively created for the Islamic tombs in China. The three eaves for the roof are actually a feature of China's traditional wooden architecture. The Eight Trigrams would indicate the eight directions that symbolize heaven and earth. With the Eight Trigrams is where the tomb is located. The whole structure of the tomb gives the architect much room for creating sculptures and brick carving—which are rich in subjects and the motifs are very lifelike. The motifs also include many symbols that relate to Han culture and traditions.

The Islamic tomb in the shape of Eight Trigrams in Linxia, Gansu.

Mosques of the Uygurs in Xinjiang

The mosques of the Uygur people are scattered in the Xinjiang regions. Since Islam was first brought into Xinjiang in the 10th century AD, they created a new architectural system as it assimilated the traditional ethnic architecture of Xinjiang.

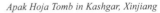
Apak Hoja Tomb in Kashgar, Xinjiang

The exterior of Id Kah Mosque in Kashgar, Xinjiang.

The deep niche in the middle of the wall of the main hall of Id Kah Mosque. The imam stands in the niche and leads the prayers to recite the Alcoran during rogation times.

The mosque of the Uygurs is fundamentally a big courtyard. The main complex is the prayer hall, with a front and a back courtyard, and it contains all the necessary features of a typical mosque such as the *mihrab*, the *qibla* and the *mimba*. The biggest and grandest mosque in Xinjiang is the Id Kah Mosque located in the central square in Kashgar City. In the prayer hall are 140 pillars, and it comprises an inner, an outer and a side hall.

The gate leads to the entrance of the mosque. From the design of the gate, one can decipher the status of the mosque in the hearts of the Uygur people. There is a screen wall that is placed between two tall minarets and the door of the mosque complex is imposing and sturdy. The artistry of the decorative ornaments found in this mosque is exquisite, displaying mastery in carving and painting art on wood, bricks and glazed tiles.

There are no idols for worshipping in the prayer hall. Instead, the ceiling, pillars and walls are decorated with verses from the

The walls of Id Kah Mosque are surrounded by carpeted corridors and worshippers kneel face to the westward walls—the direction of Mecca.

The architectural ornamentation of a Uygur mosque in Xinjiang.

Quran in calligraphic form. Among the verses are some decorative motifs, featuring various flowers and fruits. These designs are usually painted, carved out of gypsum, or are mosaic art. Others made use of glazed tiles. They are very colorful and are adorned with gold and silver powder, which added a touch of fine elegance to the style. No space is left vacant and they are filled with elaborate and exquisite patterns.

Christian Architecture

The earliest evidence of the spread of Christianity in China was first recorded in a stone tablet unearth in the Ming Dynasty in Xi'an. In it, it traced the spread of Christianity to the Tang Dynasty during the reign of Emperor Taizong in 635. At that time, Emperor Taizong adopted an open policy towards culture, which attracted the flow of culture from the diverse ethnicity in China as well as from the foreign countries. This receptive policy provided and excellent opportunity for the spread of Christianity into China. The Christian churches built during that period were oriental in their architectural style, and was called a "temple" in accordance to local Chinese custom.

From the end of the Tang Dynasty to the Northern Song Dynasty, Christianity went into oblivion in China. During the period of Yuan, it went through a period of revival and the Christian churches built during that time adopted China's traditional architectural model, with the exception of their interior.

During the Ming and the Qing dynasties, the view towards Christianity was rather erratic. At times, the government was rather relaxed with it, at other times, completely banned. Before it was banned in during the reign of Emperor Jiaqing of the Qing Dynasty, the spread of the religion was very much progressive. The Catholic Jesuit Matteo Ricci (1552–1610) arrived in Guangzhou in 1583 and he assumed the role of the president of China's Society of Jesus in 1596. Other Jesuit missionaries soon followed and arrived in China. The earliest Christian churches congregated in residences, temples or simple buildings that were of traditional Chinese style and decorated in western style, with a simple crucifix as added as a symbol. Later on, some western missionaries decided to work on their own designs, and Christian churches began to take shape within China as a foreign architecture style brought in from the West.

After 1860, under the unequal treaties signed with foreign nations, the missionaries obtained the rights to spread the Christian faith throughout the whole of China. From then on, Christian missionaries surged into China. During this period, the missionaries took on the role of conquerors as they entered into territories that were once forbidden to them. Unlike the missionaries during the times of Matteo Ricci, who believed in striking a harmonizing balance between Christianity and Chinese culture, these new missionaries advocated using Christianity to revolutionize China's culture. Reflected in the Christian churches—mainly replicas of the Western churches—in China at that time was the eclecticism in architecture common to the historical period between the end of the 19th century to the early 20th century. Given that the Catholics are more conservative, the architecture of the Catholic churches does not take on too many variations. On the other hand, the protestant churches and the eastern orthodox churches are more varied in the architectural style of their churches. In general, churches in China were mainly influence by the following models.

The earliest churches in China usually adopted this architectural style. In Shanghai, Dongjiadu Cathedral—originally named St. Xavier Cathedral—built between 1847 and 1853 is the earliest Roman-Spanish baroque style church that is still in existence. It was named after the Jesuit St. Francis Xavier, who passed away shortly before he had the chance to set foot in China. Yangjingbang Cathedral, known also as Church of St. Joseph, located at South Sichuan Road in the French settlement, was built between 1860 and 1861. It is a classical French-Roman style Catholic church adorned with an eye-catching stained-glass wall.

China's Catholic and protestant churches commonly adopted the Gothic style in their architecture and design. The Sacred Heart of Jesus Church in Guangzhou, known also as the Stone House, built between 1863 and 1888, is one the most typical and meticulously constructed Gothic-style Catholic churches in China. Its steeple, which measures 58.5 in height, is the tallest amongst all the churches in China. The most

The Xujiahui Catholic Church in Shanghai.   *St. Emile Church in Qingdao, Shandong.*

outstanding of Gothic-style churches found in China would be none other than the largest Catholic church in Shanghai, Xujiahui Cathedral, or St Ignatius Cathedral. On the sides of the main entrance are two towering belfries, and the interior of the church boasts a gothic-style framework. The loftiness and harmonizing colors of the church bring out the majestic of God's holiness, and it is no question when it is being hailed as the "Authority Figure of China's Churches". Also worth mentioning is Shanghai's earliest Christian church that is still in existence, the Holy Trinity Church—or the "Red Church" as it is known for its red bricks. It is modeled against British-Gothic style churches and is partially influenced by the Roman style.

In China, there are also a number of churches that are modeled against the Renaissance and Baroque styles. Along Zhejiang Road in Qingdao, the Catholic Church—originally named St. Emile Church—had adopted Gothicism and Romanesque and is of the neo-Romanism, a typical reflection of eclecticism in architecture. Located at a commanding point in the city center on West Haishan Hill with its pair of imposing bell towers, the church us an important structure in the city's spatial composition, as well as a popular focus of the cityscape of Qingdao.

Harbin is a city that boasts the most number of Orthodox churches in China and they were greatly influenced by Russian churches. Russian architecture is known for its fine craftsmanship and the use of gauged bricks for the walls and for other decorative elements in the building. This distinctive feature of Byzantine architecture is most apparent in Harbin's St. Sophia Church, built in 1907. The main structure of the church is laid out as a Latin Cross, and underneath its center vault are four brick buttresses supporting a circular base that measures 10 meters in diameter. On top of the circular base is a huge onion-shaped dome. And on each of the four octagonal bell towers is a tipped roof—topped with an onion-shaped dome. The bell towers vary in height in order to give prominence to the main entrance of the church.

The Christian missionaries penetrated deep into China's major cities and rural villages in their quest to spread Christianity, bringing into China the influence of Western architecture as well. Other than the major cities such as Beijing, Shanghai and Tianjin, many Western style churches can be found in rural villages that are more creative in terms of their architecture. Very often, Chinese traditional architecture structures such as pagodas, roofs, archways and decorated inner gates are blended in with Western architectural elements found in churches, such as bell towers, domes, columns, vault, rose windows and crucifix. This east-west fusion resulted in a vivid and interesting architecture model that has become a bridge between the East and the West in China's modern history.

In order to attract more converts, the missionaries were also actively involved in various cultural enterprises in cities like Shanghai, Nanjing, Tianjin, Beijing and Guangzhou, etc., such as the translation of books, the setting up of newspapers, and the founding of mission schools. They were also involved in charity works in setting up hospitals, orphanages and other charitable organizations. All these activities took place for a period of a few hundred years. Among all these works of the missionaries, the establishment of schools and hospital took on the most significant in architectural scale. The buildings of hospitals and schools were modeled against Western classicism, Eclecticism, as well as a blend of Eastern and Western elements

The colorful stained-glass window of Shanghai Moore Memorial Church.

Xi Kai Cathedral in Tianjin, built in 1916.

The Dongtang Cathedral (St. Joseph Church), one of the four largest Catholic churches in Beijing, originally built in 1655.

The Southern Catholic Church in Xuanwu District, built by Matteo Ricci during Wanli period (1573–1619) of Ming Dynasty, is the oldest church in Beijing.

or simply "Chinese style".

The earliest school building that displays the blend of East and West in its architecture is Shanghai's St. John's University's Schereschewsky Hall and other buildings in the campus. (St. John's University is the current campus of East China University of Politics and Law.) The main structure of the university building is basically western style, and the only Chinese element is found in the roofs of the various buildings that are modelled against the roofs found in Jiangnan province.

China's nationalism movement, which took place in the early 20th century, did not bring too much impact on the style adopted in building churches. Instead, it brought about the trend of exploring China's ethnic architecture style in the building of mission schools and hospitals. After the 1920s, more mission universities and hospitals took roots in China. They include Beijing's Yanjing University (today's Peking University), Nanjing's Jinling University (today's Nanjing University) and Jinling Women's University (today's Nanjing Normal University campus), Guangzhou's Lingnan University (today's Sun Yat-sen University) and Beijing's Union Hospital. These college buildings and hospitals fully exemplify western architects' knowledge and understanding of China's traditional architecture, as well as their grasp of the constituent in applying western architectural design methods in rendering Chinese traditional architecture (mainly for the roof). Even though the trials undertaken by these architects were built on architectural models based on western ideologies, but the legacy they left behind brings enlightenment to the many Chinese architects that continue to make new discoveries in the same field.

Appreciation of Chinese Gardens

West Garden in Suzhou.

China's classical gardens were known for blending nature and man-made features in order to create a relaxing environment where one could roam freely in. They combined the best of architecture, painting, literature, and horticulture— making them the most integrated architecture form that boasts the highest level of artistry.

The classical gardens found in China can be divided into three major categories. The imperial gardens were meant for the emperors and their families. These gardens were usually part of the imperial palaces, the temporary abodes and palaces away from the capital where the emperors stayed for short periods. These gardens were massive in scale and were meant for the emperors' short stay, leisure, entertainment and hunting activities, as well as for the consecration of gods and deities. Private gardens were mainly built in the cities or in the outskirts of the cities, and they were also part of the residences. Though they were of a much smaller scale as compared to the imperial gardens, they were of an elegant style and were exquisitely constructed. They were usually for the literati to enjoy some quiet moments, for scholars to socialize with one another, or for high officials and rich merchants to display their social status and wealth. Then, there were the gardens that were built against the natural landscape, where there were abundant greenery and sources of water. These were usually combined with man-made structures and were open to the public.

Other gardens were found in Buddhist monasteries, Taoist temples and ancestral temples. These gardens were usually located in scenic areas where there were dense forests so as to create a tranquil environment within and outside the temple grounds. Some of these gardens can be found in some well-known temples across China. For instance, Tantuo Temple and Jietai Temple in Beijing, the Jin Ancestral Hall in Taiyuan of Shanxi Province, Xi Garden in Suzhou of Jiangsu Province, Lingyin Temple in Hangzhou of Zhejiang Province, and Eight Outer Temples in Chengde of Hebei Province. They are all of varying scales. Some of them are as big as the imperial gardens, or can be as small as a private garden. They are mostly set again natural landscapes, which are also tourist spots that open to all visitors.

Imperial Gardens

Imperial gardens are the earliest Chinese classical gardens and they are found in almost all the dynasties of China. They belong exclusively to the emperors and the imperial families and were usually created out of natural landscape, with man-made structures added to them to bring out the grandeur of the imperial family. With his political and economic privileges, the emperor could take ownership of any big plot of land and make it into a garden for his own leisure enjoyment. Surpassing any private gardens in size, the smallest imperial gardens could easily occupy an area of several hundred acres, with the biggest measuring up to several hundred miles.

The earliest recorded imperial gardens in China were built in 11th century B.C during the Shang Dynasty and Zhou Dynasty. The existing imperial gardens in China were all constructed or rebuilt during the Qing Dynasty. The beautifully landscaped imperial gardens of the Qing Dynasty emphasize on their functional values and the choice of names of the scenic spots within them. This brought about a unique feature seen in most

The Outer Eight Temples of the Summer Palace in Chengde.

Bird's eye view of the Summer Palace in Chengde.

imperial gardens with the combination of beautiful landscaped gardens and imperial palaces. The most representative of such imperial gardens would be the summer palace in Chengde and Beijing's Summer Palace (Yihe Garden) and Old Summer Palace (Yuanming Garden).

Summer Palaces in Chengde—"Miniature of the World for the Emperor"

Landscape of Jiangnan in the Summer Palace in Chengde.

In the early period of the Qing Dynasty, Emperor Kangxi had a summer palace built in Chengde. This was primarily for the purpose of strengthening the political ties with Mongolia, as well as to unite the various ethnic groups in the country. It was not simply a garden estate for the emperor and his family to escape the scorching heat in the capital, but also a political command center.

The design of the summer palace gave prominence to and conveyed the idea of the imposing authority of the emperor. Beyond the palace grounds, the main garden in the summer palace estate can be divided into three categories—the lake scenic spot, the plain scenic spot, and the mountainous scenic spot—

which combine the sceneries of northern and southern China. The scenery around the lake is rich in the flavor of Jiangnan's regions of lakes and rivers, the plain reminds one of the open plains in the regions beyond the Great Wall, and the mountainous scenery is like a replica of the mountains in the north. Such replicas were not mere plagiarisms; they were skillfully designed and recreated so as to enable the palaces within the garden estate to blend in with the sceneries of the common people.

Once the men of letters started participating in the design of the landscape gardens, the pursuit of artistic moods became the chief characteristic of China's landscaped gardens. There were many talented poets and painters among the many outstanding landscape designers, especially during the periods of the Ming and Qing dynasties, where most of the well-known gardens were entirely designed by the painter. In the Qing Dynasty, the task of designing the imperial gardens was undertaken by members of the imperial institution of paintings. Even then, the imperial gardens were still man-made sceneries, and it was impossible to realistically present true, natural beauty to the visitors. The level of appreciation of the garden scenery was very much a reflection of the visitors' aesthetic tastes and their cultural background.

The Map of the Summer Palace, *drawn by Qing artist, Leng Mei.*

Yuanming Garden (The Old Summer Palace) —"Garden of all Gardens"

To the northwest of Beijing is the old summer palace, Yuanming Garden—took 200 years to complete under the directions of the Qing Dynasty emperors Kangxi, Yongzheng, Qianlong, Jiaqing, Daoguang and Xianfeng. It is the only one of its kind in all the dynasties in China, and was a large summer palace estate composed of three gardens—Yuanming Garden, Changchun Garden and Qichun Garden.

All the three gardens of the old summer palace were lakes and rivers parks. The garden was primarily designed with lakes and rivers as the main theme. Sceneries of lakes and rivers occupied 69 spots in Yuanming Garden, and 54 spots in Changchun Garden and Qichun Garden. Among them, the more prominent scenic spots were named by the emperors. Within

The landscape of Jiuzhou Qingyan (Tranquility and Peace of Chinese Nation) in the Old Summer Palace is the place where emperors to invite parties. Destroyed by the French-British allied army in a fire in 1860.

each of these 120 or more scenic spots were smaller gardens, which were interconnected with a network of river system and footpaths. These small gardens would gradually extend to the bigger garden. With such skillful rendering, visitors to the small gardens would feel as if they were walking through different environments of unending space. Owing to this unique feature, Yuangming Garden was hailed as the "garden of all gardens".

During the end of the Ming Dynasty and the early Qing Dynasty, the missionary work of the Catholics was already very much in progress and a few of them actually took part in the design of the old summer palace. They included the French missionaries Benoist Michael (1715–1774) and Jear Lenis Attiet (1702–1768), the Italian missionary Giuseppe Castiglione (1688–1766) and the Bohemian missionary Lgatuis Sickeltart (1708–1780). Together, they designed six 18th century Baroque style palaces and gardens, and they were termed the "Western Mansions"—a unique sight to behold in the old Summer Palace. These European-style western palaces were the first complete work that was ever built in China. They were also the first work that successfully combined both European and Chinese architectural styles in landscaped garden.

The Old Summer Palace inherited China's 3000 years'

heritage constructing landscape gardens. It exuded the magnificent elegance of a palace building, and the charms of Jiangnan's water landscape. It had even assimilated the architecture models of designing European-style gardens, and combined diverse architectural elements of landscaped garden as a whole. It was known not only as a garden of all gardens, but also an imperial museum that boasts an amazing collection. The French author Victor Hugo (1802–1885) once commented that even when all the rare treasures in France were to be put together, it would not match the scale and splendour of this oriental museum. Sadly, the Old Summer Palace was destroyed by the French-British legions in a fire in 1860. Today, the ruins could only offer a tiny glimpse into the original work of art.

The relic of the Old Summer Palace, Beijing.

Yihe Garden (The Summer Palace)—The Last Imperial Garden

The Summer Palace is another representative of Qing Dynasty's imperial garden. Occupying a land area of 290 hectares, it is the only existing and most well preserved ancient garden in China.

Fuoxiang Pavilion (Pavilion of the Fragrance of Buddha) of the Summer Palace, Beijing.

Long Corridor of the Summer Palace, Beijing.

The Summer Palace was originally built in the year 1750 and was named Qingyi Garden. Its overall design was based on Hangzhou's West Lake and was greatly influence by the designs of landscaped gardens of Jiangnan. Like Yuanming Garden, it was destroyed in a fire in 1860. The then ruler of the Qing imperial court, Empress Dowager Cixi (Dragon Empress) had used navy funds to rebuilt the garden, and it was renamed The Summer Palace. Upon its restoration, it became the temporary abode and political center of Cixi, who stayed there for long periods of time.

Lakes and rivers are important elements of a garden. The choice of location for The Summer Palace was based on this concept. With Kunming Lake as its center, three islands were constructed in the lake—a classic layout popular at the time. The Summer Palace is the only last surviving imperial garden built on this model.

Building Buddhist monasteries, Taoist temples and ancestral temples in the imperial gardens is one of its distinctive characteristics. This is especially so for Buddhist temples, which took up the majority in such buildings. Almost all the imperial gardens had at least one Buddhist temple built within them. Emperor Qianlong had

Qingyi Garden built as a birthday present to the Empress Dowager. Hence, the focal point of the garden would be the group of buildings that constituted Longevity Temple in front of Wanshoushan (Longevity Hill). This group of buildings comprised different halls and was built along an axis from the foot of the hill to the mountainside. And one of the halls, Fuoxiang Pavilion (Pavilion of the Fragrance of Buddha), which is located at the highest platform, would be the symbol of the Summer Palace and it is the center of the entire garden.

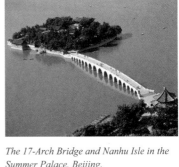

The 17-Arch Bridge and Nanhu Isle in the Summer Palace, Beijing.

During the reigns of Kangxi and Qianlong, there were unceasing wars taking place along the border regions. In order to unite the Mongolians and the Tibetans, who are Buddhists, Emperor Qianlong built a Lama temple against the model of Tibet's ancient temple Samye Temple at the back of Longevity Hill. On one of the island in the lake—Nanhu Isle—there was also a temple that consecrates the Dragon King, and it was called Guangrun Temple.

Using natural landscape as a backdrop of gardens is an important technique that was commonly used in designing China's ancient gardens. This technique is fully exemplifies in the design of the Summer Palace. When standing at the platform inform of Pavilion of the Fragrance of Buddha, one can see the mountain range of the West Hills, the reflection of Yuquan Hill

Suzhou Street of the Summer Palace, Beijing.

on the lake, and admire the green of Kunming Lake and the mist that hangs over West Embankment. All these natural blend in with the buildings in the garden to form a picturesque view.

Another well-known feature in the Summer Palace is the Long Corridor. It is located to the southern foothill of Longevity Hill. The Long Corridor measures 728 meters in length and has 8,000 over paintings illustrated in it. The Long Corridor stretches from the north of Kunming Lake right to the west of it, forming a link between the natural landscape and the buildings in the garden.

One can see many beautiful sights of Jiangnan in the Summer Palace. To begin with, The Summer Palace was designed with Jiangnan's West Lake in mind. It is very much a replica of West Lake. The area behind the lake has a Suzhou Street, which is built on the models of the streets in Suzhou and Nanjing. This folk art in creating landscape garden greatly adds a refreshing touch to the imperial gardens.

The Summer Palace is a marvelous work of landscaping art that combines different unique features of landscaped gardens. It exudes the splendor and majesty of an imperial compound and the exquisite elegance of folk architecture. It is indeed a rare gem of China's landscaped garden artistry.

Private Gardens

The owners of private gardens were usually retired court officials, men of letters, landlords and rich merchants. China's ancient etiquette system enforced restrictions on the lifestyle and spending of the common people. Anyone who went

Section of Yule Pavilion (Happy Fish Pavilion) in Yuyuan Garden, Shanghai.

Yuyuan Garden in Shanghai.

Chinese Architecture

Zhuozheng Garden (Humble Administrator's Garden) in Suzhou.

against the regulations would be prosecuted. As such, the private gardens were unmatchable in its scale and style to the imperial gardens.

Chinese classical gardens flourished from the periods of Wei, Jin and the North-South dynasties. During this period, the men of letters were tired of war and seek pleasures in nature and prided themselves in elegance and style—becoming the forerunners of the men of letters in later years. Richness in poetic and artistic flavor became a signature pursuit of what they wanted to see in gardens. The German philosopher Georg Wilhelm Friedrich Hegel (1770–1831) once described a Chinese garden as a painting that is natural and rich in poetic style. It is unlike any gardens found in the popular French botanical style— following the strict geometrical composition model of the ancient Roman, which emphasized on the principle of creating an imposing scale.

From the middle of the Ming Dynasty to the end of the Qing Dynasty, Jiangnan became a centralized place of private gardens, with the trend of landscaped gardens in vogue for over 300 years. This could be attributed to the fact that Jiangnan has an abundant source of water and variety of plants, a temperate climate and rich in soil and minerals. Other than these factors, Jiangnan's society was rich and populous, and most importantly, an

Geyuan Garden in Yangzhou.

Yuyuan Garden in Shanghai.

Deyue Pavilion in Suzhou.

The sketched map of rockeries and pavilions.

increasing number of men of letters and artists had all participated in the design of its gardens. All these ensure a high expertise in the art of landscaping gardens. At that time, the most prominent figures in the art of landscaping gardens was the theoretician Ji Cheng (1582–?) and the landscape artist Zhang Lian (1587–1671). They were both contemporaries of the European representative landscape designer, Andre Le Notre (1613–1700)—famed for his design of the gardens of Vaux-le-Vicomte and Versailles.

Private gardens were usually modeled against the requirements and interests of the owners. As private gardens occupied a small space, and in order to create a unique style to the taste of the owner, the garden designer had to be very creative in making use of the limited space in constructing a garden with wide varieties to satisfy the pleasure of the visitors. One excellent example would be Suzhou's Lingering Garden.

Making use of natural scenery is also an important tactic

employed by the landscape designer when designing a garden. This involves skillfully using the faraway natural landscape as the background of the garden.

Creating artificial hills and channeling water are two techniques that are vital to designing Chinese gardens. One reason is because they can be excellent imitations of natural landscape, and secondly it represents the yearning for virtue and wisdom.

In creating artificial hills, one does not seek the greatness in scale, but a refinement of all the elements attached to a natural landscape. The best materials used in the making of artificial hills are stones taken from the lakes. They are choice materials because of the smoothness and the exquisite brightness of the stones that are polished by water over a long period of time, as well as their natural contours. The most famous of such stones is none other than the ones from Tai Lake and they are known as "Tai Lake Stones".

The water surfaces in the garden are designed in irregular layout so as to bear resemblances to the natural landscape. The rivers and lakes are usually accompanied with artificial mountains to create an uneven and natural touch to an otherwise man-made garden. Other than hills and plants, building such as

The Four-seasons Rockeries in Geyuan Garden in Yangzhou.

107

pavilions, corridors and bridges are also important to a garden. They serve as the subjects in the composition of a garden and constitute the scenic spots in it.

Chinese classical arts, especially poetry and paintings, had greatly influenced the designs of landscaped gardens. On the other hand, poets and artists also obtained their creative inspirations from the tranquil sights offered by a beautifully landscaped garden. Arts and landscaped gardens compliment each other in their glories. One example of private gardens would have to be Zhuozheng Garden (Humble Administrator's Garden) in Suzhou. It was built in the middle of Ming Dynasty, and spans a history of more than 500 years. The famous Ming artist Wen Zhengming (1470–1559) had several painting inspired by this garden.

To many scholars and literati, their material and spiritual lives were inseparable from the landscape gardens. In a landscaped garden, one could also feel the emotions and interests of these individuals. A landscape garden is not merely composed with artificial hills, rivers and pavilions. It is a work of art that is put together with different artistries that exist in China's culture and society.

Zhuozheng Garden (Humble Administrator's Garden) in Suzhou.

Vernacular Dwellings

Vernacular dwellings of China refers to the indigenous architectural styles that have their roots in the rustic landscape, and centers on residential houses, and includes structures such as ancestral temples, opera houses, and memorial gateways. The origination and development of China's local architecture are closely related to the society and lifestyle of the people. They are also reflective of people's state of production, customs and habits, ethnic differences, religious beliefs; at the same time, an accumulation of people's aesthetic orientation and social awareness.

Patriarchal ideology and moral principles, as well as the doctrines of *yin-yang* and the five elements have a far-reaching influence on the external and internal layouts and the creation of space in China's traditional local architecture. China's traditional residence has its roots in adapting to the need and tradition where generations live under the same roof. From ethnic villages, fortified villages, dwellings of common ancestry and clan courtyard houses—they were all built on the bond of blood relations. As the Chinese people attached great significance to the tradition of honoring their ancestors, hence the ancestral temple, where the ancestors are revered, is often the most important building in a household, or even an entire village, and it is the center around which other buildings are built.

The concept of *li* (respect) in China's ancient patriarchal system and ethical codes is centered on the relationship between father and son, the order of seniority, and the social differences between men and women. In terms of the layout of a residence, the room that belongs to the parents—known as the principal room—is placed in the center along the axis of the house. The wing-rooms, which are occupied by children and grandchildren, would be situated in the eastern and western sides of the principal room. Such difference is also apparent in the difference sizes of the buildings and their interior design and decorations. In distinguishing the difference between men and women, women was bound by many restrictions and not given much personal freedom. As reflected in the interior of a residential compound, men's quarters are placed in the outer courtyard, whereas for the women, in the inner courtyard. In general, women were not allowed to step out of their inner compound without being given the permission to do so. The same applied for outsiders; they were not to step into the inner compound.

Feng Shui (Geomantic omen) is a school of geomancy based on China's ancient doctrine of the five elements—used in deciphering the best locations for building a residence and burial. The ancient Chinese believed that a building's *feng shui* could greatly influence the prosperity and development of a family, hence it was the first thing that must be considered when choosing the location of a house, in designing its layout and in the creation of space within the house.

China has a large territory and a wide spectrum of ethnic groups. The varied natural landscapes and ethnic customs give rise to a colorful and rich characteristic in the various architectural styles that are apparent in residences all across China. These residences are not only unique in its building structure, but are also wide in variety.

Beijing *Siheyuan* Building (Courtyard Houses)

In Northern China, one major characteristic of the traditional residential houses is the courtyard, which is the center of the house. A courtyard house is built on the basic principle of having a firm, solid exterior blend in with a vacant, spacious interior. The house is constructed on an invisible axis, around which the

The main gate of Beijing siheyuan *(courtyard houses) building.*

The aisle of a courtyard house.

different functional rooms are built. Beijing's courtyard houses (*siheyuan* in Chinese) were predominantly situated within the capital city. Its architectural structure fit perfectly into the official model that was typical in the capital, which deemed it necessary to fulfill certain religious and moral principles that were essential to maintaining order in a traditional family.

A typical Beijing courtyard house employed an invisible north-south axis when designing the layout of the house. The main gate of the house would be placed at the southeastern corner of the house. In accordance to principles of *feng shui* and the Eight Trigrams, this is considered the most auspicious direction and could bring wealth to the household. Upon entering the house, one is greeted by an exquisitely crafted screen wall, which, in the past, carried the function of warding off evil spirits. It also helps in creating space and maintaining one's privacy.

A turn to the west of the main gate would be a small and narrow front yard. To the south of the courtyard are the living room, study, accounts room and storage room. To the north of the front yard is the second and inner gate of the compound, which is also situated along the axis. The two festoon pillars at its sides are exquisitely carved with elaborate floral designs, making it the most prominent design element in the entire courtyard compound. The festoon gate acts as a divider between the outer and inner courtyards. Behind the festoon gate is the main living compound of the courtyard house. Here, the courtyard is beautifully landscaped with trees and other plants, creating a tranquil and comfortable living environment. To the north of the courtyard, the south-facing principal room makes up the main building of the courtyard house. And in accordance to Ming and Qing building regulations for residential houses, there are usually three rooms—with two side rooms flanking the principal room. At both sides of courtyard are the wing-rooms. Behind the principal room, there is a small courtyard, with a row of rooms forming the last section of the courtyard compound.

Within a courtyard compound, all the rooms are assigned to the members of the family according to seniority. The principal rooms are for the senior members of the household. Within the principal room, an altar and the ancestor tablet are put in place. The side rooms are for the junior members. For the other rooms in the house, they must not surpass the principal rooms in terms of their areas, heights and interior decoration. This gives prominence to the idea of showing respect to the ancestors and

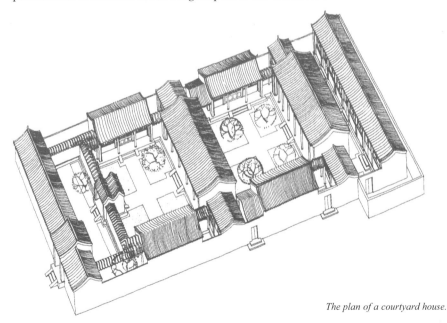

The plan of a courtyard house.

acknowledging the power and influence of the patriarch. This makes the principal room not only the main activity room of the family, but also a symbol of the family's spirit.

One advantage of a courtyard house is that it could be infinitely expanded. As the number of family members increases, more rooms can be added, with more courtyards created. More courtyards and rooms can also be built beyond the existing compound, with corridors and walls connecting the annexes to the main compound. This construction mode for residential houses is in keeping with China's ancient family tradition and its development.

Other than those in Beijing, the courtyard houses in south Hebei, Shanxi, Shaanxi, Henan, etc. are long and narrow built in the north-south direction, as it is hot during the summer, and hence helps in shedding the interior of the house from the strong sunlight. In the northwestern provinces, such as Gansu and Qinghai, the houses have thick and high walls to keep away sand and protect from the cold weather. In the northeastern provinces, where the land is vast with small population, and a weather that is often cold, there is the need to maximize the intake of sunlight. Hence, the houses there are usually big and spacious. Thus, in various places in China, the courtyard houses take on different characteristics in accordance to the environments they are in.

Northwestern Cave Dwelling

Cave dwelling is a residence that is attached with the earth and is fully in tune with nature conservation. It does not have the typical form or outline found in ordinary buildings. It exhibits an artistic aura—the natural yellow of the earth, its rough texture and its creation of living space in the cave's interior. It is rough, unsophisticated and rich in local flavor. There are three main categories of cave dwellings: those built in the cliff, in the earth, and with stone.

Cave dwellings that are built in the cliff were created out of a horizontal cave. They are set at the foot of a hill and along a ditch and undulated in height. Given the thickness of the cave walls, a hole can also be dug above the existing cave to create a "sky cave", which allows sunlight into the cave. The cave can be connected to the surface with a slope, brick steps, or an indoor staircase. Outside the cave dwelling is usually a small courtyard enclosed within a mud wall. It could also be joined with a stone cave dwelling to form a big courtyard house.

Courtyard cave dwelling is created by digging deep into the ground—forming a sunken courtyard in the ground. Then in the four walls, caves are dug to create rooms. The courtyard cave is linked to the surface by way of a long staircase, which could be placed either within the courtyard or built through the earth. The staircase comes in all kinds of design, adding a delightful touch to the cluster of courtyard cave dwellings.

Stone cave dwellings are constructed using bricks and stones. The most common design of stone cave dwelling is the three-cavity cave dwelling, which also formed the basic unit of a courtyard compound. It can also be connected with a wooden house, with the stone cave dwelling functioning as the best room because it is warm in winter and cool in summer.

Although the architectural style of cave dwellings are far from the conventional residential houses, in terms of the combination of space it still retains the traditional layout of a Chinese household. The northern portion of the cave dwelling still functions as the family dayroom and also exclusively used as the bedroom of the most senior members of the family. The side rooms in the eastern and western ends of the house are still used as bedrooms, kitchen and storeroom of the house. The southern side is where the entrance to the house is located and also where one finds the toilet and the livestock pen. The main gate to the courtyard is constructed at the southeastern corner of the house. Hence, there are many resemblances in layout to a typical

Courtyard cave dwellings in Shan County, Henan.

115

Multi-layered cave dwellings in Shijiagou, Shanxi.

courtyard house. From this, we can see how far-reaching the impact of ancient feudal society is, regardless of the different styles and materials used in constructing a residential dwelling.

Huizhou Dwellings

Huizhou is an area strong in traditional family values and the people there attach great significance to *feng shui* in selecting a spot to build a house. People who share the same surnames formed clans and live together as a community. The

ancestral temple, which formed the core of the community, is where sacrificial rites and ceremonies and other clan activities are held. This results in a community that is bonded, literally, by blood. Generations of people of this same clan built their houses around the ancestral temple.

The landscape of Hong Village in Yi County, Anhui.

The typical residential dwelling of Huizhou employs the layout of a courtyard house. This building structure is popular in the regions of Jiangsu, Zhejiang, Anhui, and Jiangxi. In general, when one enters through the main gate, he is greeted by a courtyard, which forms the center of the residence. All the rooms at the four sides of the courtyard would drain water towards the courtyard. This is symbolic in the sense that money, which is symbolized by water, will not flow out of the house. Next, one will see a partly opened main hall, flanked by side rooms. Behind the main hall are the staircase and the kitchen. The staircase can also be set in the space between the main hall and the side room. Connected by a corridor, the layout of the second level is exactly the same as the ground level. The residence is surrounded by high walls that are lined with green tiles—adding an aesthetic touch to the entire compound.

The details of woodcut in Huizhou vernacular dwellings.

117

White walls with cascading small roofs are called "Horsehead Wall".

Huizhou is populated with merchants. The richly ornamented residences of the wealthy merchants were also used for displaying the power and wealth of the owners. In fact, residences in Huizhou are well known for their wood, brick and stone carvings. In order to prevent fire from spreading into their own compounds, or vice versa, the people in Huizhou built high wall in their compounds for the purpose of blocking fire. From this practice, the art of decorating the walls is being derived. The undulating walls of the houses in Huizhou exemplify the uniqueness of the residences themselves.

Upland Dwellings in Sichuan-Chongqing Region

Sichuan-Chongqing region is located in the southwest of China and has enjoyed a long history in its culture. It is an area that is densely populated and has a precipitous terrain. Hence the residences in Sichuan-Chongqing region are linked across the uneven terrain. In terms of the building's layout, there is still the existence of the axis in the main complex of the house—

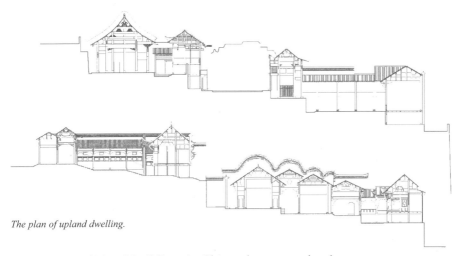

The plan of upland dwelling.

as in most traditional buildings in China—but not so for the secondary complexes and the courtyard. The houses in this region are built to adapt to the physical features of the land. And there are a few distinctive features:

Terrace: This is applied on steep mountainside, where a level shelf of land interrupting a declivity is constructed, like a flight of steps. The houses can thus be built on the terraces. And from afar, is an amazing sight to behold.

Balcony: Applied to narrow space in a terrain for the purpose of expanding the space of an interior, usually for a room at the second level. Additional space is created by adding a balcony to the selected room.

Steps: Applied on the portion of a hillside where it is flat, the house is built perpendicular to the natural incline of the slope. This is usually used in building a residence's side rooms.

Slope: Houses are also built perpendicular to the incline of the slope. Used on a hillside that is not as steep as the one for "Steps". This is solely to separate the floors of the interior of the house into different heights.

Annex: This involves extending the back of the roof and creating annexes to the existing house. This is usually used to extend the space of the side rooms. The annexes built may become much lower than the existing side rooms.

Hanging room: As it is difficult to increase the depth of the

The riverside topography of Chongqing area determines the architectural style of vernacular dwellings.

119

house when building it on a slope, a room is added by having it built to suspend or hang off from a room in the upper level to create more space. The hanging room can also function as an awning for the entrance located at the ground level. Such hanging rooms can be found in Chongqing, near the Yangtze River, or along the cost of Jialing River.

Earthen Houses of Fujian

Many Hakka earthen houses can be found in the south Fujian regions of Yongding, Longyan, Zhangping and Zhangzhou. The earthen houses are usually huge—each has 3 to 4 levels and reaches up to 13 meters in height. The outer walls, which are one to two meters thick, are made of clay and are very sturdy. These uniquely designed earthen houses are regarded as architectural gems of China's residences. The three most symbolic types of earthen houses are the round earthen houses, rectangular earthen houses and the *Wufeng* (Five Phoenixes) earthen houses.

The people that built the earthen houses were the Hakkas, a group of Han Chinese. During the periods of Wei and Jin, they migrated southwards due to wars and unrests. At that time, the society was unstable, and robbery and theft were rampant. The earthen houses facilitated the tradition living together in one community as an ethnic clan, and each of these fortress-like

The earthen house group in Chuxi, Fujian.

houses can accommodate a few hundreds people. The earthen house was a perfect defense against attacks and trespasses.

The Hakkas have their roots in the central plains of China. Most of the first Hakkas that migrated south were scholars and officials from well-to-do families. It is a heritage that the Hakkas are still very proud of today. Even though their culture has changed along with history, it is a culture that is closely linked to Chinese culture and tradition that is still strongly influenced by China's feudal system and propriety.

Zhencheng House in Yongding, Fujian, built in 1912.

The most representative of the circular earthen houses is Chengqi Building—located in Yongding County in the Fujian province. Chengqi Building was built in the Qing Dynasty during the 48th year of Emperor Kangxi's reign in 1709. It took three years to build and has a diameter of 62.6 meters. Chengqi Building contains four concentric rings. The outer ring has four levels, with the ground level used as the kitchen, the second level used as a store, and the third and fourth levels as bedrooms. Every level is connected with a corridor. The second and third rings are single-level houses, and the entire innermost building is used as the ancestral hall, which is laid against the axis, along which the main gate is also situated.

For rectangular earthen houses, all the four sides of the house are three to four stories high. In the inner courtyard of the house and along the axis is where the ancestral hall is situated. In general, annexes are added within the periphery of the house and its inner courtyard, and they blend in extremely well with the earthen building—displaying the relationship between the principal and the subordinate. They are an indispensable part of the entire building structure and create a richly colorful spatial form and an elegant image in the colony of houses.

The interior of Qiaofu House in Yongding, Fujian.

The ancestral hall placed right in the center of the rectangular earthen houses is for the consecration of the ancestor's tablet and where sacrificial ceremonies are held. In the community, the ancestral hall is held in utmost reverence. Respecting the ancestors is a traditional value and a tie that binds kinship. Placing the ancestral hall right in the center of the inner courtyard of the house is not only in accordance to the ritual system of

The inner ring of Chengqi House in Yongding, Fujian.

Section of an earthen house.

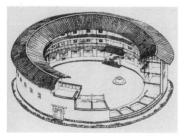

worship, but also—for the many Hakka migrants into Fujian—a meaningful connection to their roots.

The *Wufeng* building is a prominent style amongst the earthen houses. Three main halls are built along the axis. The lower hall is where the entrance is located and it is lower in terms of height. The central hall is the ancestral hall. It is used for receiving guests and for holding clan ceremonies. It is the center of the entire house and it is built higher than the rest of the houses in the house. The rear hall is the main hall comprising three to five levels—towering towards the northern end of the axis. It is the tallest building of the entire house and where the elder members of the family reside. The three halls are connected via corridors, which formed two courtyards.

The *Wufeng* in the name refer to five birds of different colors—

red, yellow, green, violet and white. They also denotes five directions—north, south, east, west and center—meaning that the house has an axis and forms a whole with its left, right, front and back. From the exterior, the *Wufeng* building is multi-layered—resembling a grand palace as well as a phoenix that is about to take off into the sky.

Wufeng (Five Phoenixes) earthen house in Fujian.

The *Wufeng* building is the earliest earthen house that appeared in Fujian. Hence, it is most closely related to the traditional building structures in the central plains in China. Gradually, it evolved into the rectangular earthen house and the round earthen house, which in most of them, the only thing that still connects it to traditional family values is the place of the ancestral hall within the house itself. This is most obvious for the circular houses. Other than the ancestral hall, which is held in great reverence, the rooms are assigned to the members of the household randomly, regardless of their seniority, the direction the room is facing or the position it is in. In the Five-Phoenixes building, the traditional ethical principals are in full swing. In this house, one can see that the layout of the house is representative of ethical principals and Confucius thinking.

Ancient Chinese society had many strict regulations that applied to the construction of residential houses. They are mainly to distinguish between the houses of the common people from the wealthy officials. These regulations ranged from the layout of the house to its decorative aspect. The earthen houses are grand and magnificent—the scale of which easily surpassed many residences of the common people. The architectural style itself and its décor are in clear defiance again the regulations set by the different governments that the common people were to adhere to. So how did they come into existence? One reason could be due their locations. Fujian's southwestern regions are rural areas and were far from the reach of the authorities. Another reason is that the existing earthen houses were constructed in the Qing Dynasty and this reflected how the displeasure the Hakkas (who are Han Chinese) displayed against the Manchu government.

Built out of earth into such massive looking fortress-like

The interior of a Mongolian Yurt.

houses, and having being in existence for a few hundred years while retaining its past glories, the earthen houses are awe-inspiring. To have a big family of a few hundred households all living harmoniously under one roof and living as a united community against attacks from external forces is something that wins praises all round.

The Mongolian Yurt

The Mongolian yurt is a circular domed dwelling that is usually four to six meters in diameter. It consists of a wooden frame supporting a felt cover. At the top of the yurt is a movable ceiling, which can be opened to allow sunlight and ventilation in the yurt. Inside the yurt, the living area is situated close to the entrance, with the fireplace right in the center of the yurt. On the ground and the walls are colorful felt rugs that make the whole interior a cosy dwelling space—despite its small space.

The Mongolians are nomads and they usually move about twice within a year. In May when the weather is warm, they go in search of a spot with ample water supply and green pastures for grazing their livestock. In October when the weather gets cold, they would go in search of a warmer place to spend winter. The yurt is a portable structure that requires a couple of hours to take down. It would then be transported using a camel or house driven cart.

Mongolian Yurt.

Xinjiang's Aywang

Aywang is a Uygur word that means "where brightness resides". It is also the name of a dwelling typical of the Uygurs in Xinjiang. Aywang is a popular architectural style in Xinjiang and it got its name from Aywang Hall. It exhibits a distinctive ethnic quality of the Uygurs and is also representative of the region of Xinjiang.

Aywang Hall is the largest, tallest, best decorated, and brightest of such residences. Inside the hall, there are 8 columns that extend out of the ceiling, with high windows to allow sunlight into the hall. Around the columns are raised platforms for all the daily activities from work to play. On festive occasions, it becomes an open space for the Uygur people to celebrate with songs and dances. Aywang Hall thus becomes the model by which all the other rooms in an aywang are built.

Inside of a Uygur folk residence in Xinjiang.

From an architectural perspective, an aywang is entirely an interior of a building, which is also the living room of a residence. But in terms of its functions, it can be regarded as an outdoor venue for entertaining guests, holding gatherings, and music and activities. The aywang is a perfect building that best fit the weather conditions in their regions, shielding the inhabitants against sandstorms, cold, and the harsh weather in summer. Hence it is a residence that is built based on the geographical and culture landscapes of the inhabitants. The distinctive weather

The Old City of Kashgar, Xinjiang.

conditions of Xinjiang would be source of inspiration to the Uygurs in creating the aywang.

The interior of the Uygur residence is neat and presentable. Its walls are decorated with woven objects such as woven curtains and wall felts, and the floor is carpeted. To obtain heat, there is fireplace or fire pit, which does not dirty or pollute house easily. The Uygurs commonly use gypsum as material in creating decorative designs on the walls, eaves and mihrab.

Tibetan Stone Houses

The Tibetan people are mainly scattered across the regions of Tibet, Qinghai, Gansu and west of Sichuan. In order to adapt to the weather conditions and environment in the Qinghai-Tibet plateau, the Tibetans traditionally built fortress-like stone houses.

A Tibetan stone house usually comprises three to four levels. The ground level is where livestock, fodder and other items are stored. On the second level are the bedrooms and kitchen. The third level is where the prayer room is situated. As Tibetans are

Fortress-like stone house in Tibetan areas.

Buddhist, the prayer room for the recitation of Buddhist scriptures is an important part of a Tibetan home. It is placed at the topmost level as no one is to reside or nothing is to be placed above the altar. To create more space in the house, the second level is frequently extended beyond the existing walls. With annexes added to the house, the exterior of the stone house takes on many changes.

The colors of the Tibetan stone houses are simple, yet well coordinated, and usually comprise primary colors such as yellow, cream, beige and maroon—set against the brightly colored walls and roofs. The walls are created out of coarse stones and have windows of various sizes—in a descending order from the top of the wall. On every window is a colorful eave. Viewed against the blue sky, white clouds and the shimmering white of the snow mountains and glaciers, these colorful stone houses take on a rough and yet dignified style.

The Bamboo Houses of Dai Ethnic Group in Yunnan

The Dai is an ancient ethnic minority that resides in the Yunnan's Xishuangbanna Dai Autonomous Prefecture and Dehong Dai and Jingpo Autonomous Prefecture. It is an area with an abundance of bamboo woods.

The Dai villages are scattered in the vast plains or alongside the river, in order to facilitate production and allow easy access to water source. The Dai are predominantly Hinayana Buddhist

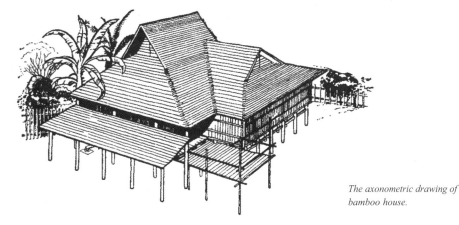

The axonometric drawing of bamboo house.

Dai villages in Yunnan.

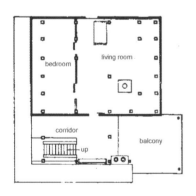

The plan of bamboo house.

and still hold on to some forms of ancient indigenous religion. At every street that leads to the village or on high grounds, one can see many uniquely designed Buddhist temples and pagodas.

In the village, every household has its individual house, which is surrounded by bamboo fences and within which fruit trees and other plants are cultivated. The houses are generally constructed using bamboo. Hence they are called "bamboo houses". The houses generally takes on a rectangular shape and are raised on stilts above the ground to create a space underneath the house for keeping livestock and for storage, as well as for ventilation.

The influence of religion and ancestor worship on the architectural style of the Dai people adds a colorful touch to the public buildings in the Dai villages. The red, white and gold of the temples and pagodas create a refreshing contrast to the plain yet elegant residences.

Architectural Ornamentation

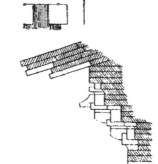

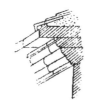

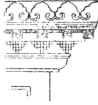

The different materials and styles of eaves in traditional Chinese architecture.

Several popular forms of corbel brackets in ancient China.

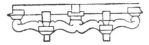

The ancient Chinese architectural system was based on the wooden structural framework, and to a relatively large extent, contemporary Chinese architectural styles are still very much defined by wooden structures. The ancient Chinese artisans fully understood and therefore maximized the special qualities of timber structures, through the use of instruments such as knives, hammers and chisels, drills and brushes, working their compositions and artistic adornments directly on the timber. These craftsmen also applied the traditional Chinese arts of painting, carving, calligraphy, colors, motifs and patterns in architectural ornamentation, in order to accentuate the expressiveness of art in architecture. As such, architectural ornamentation was an important element of ancient Chinese architectural styles.

Ancient Chinese architectural ornamentation could be divided into three categories, namely, gold ornaments (made from materials like metals, jade etc.), colorful ornamentation (brushstrokes, paintings and murals) and carvings (floral motifs, embossment and sculptures). Some common factors which linked these ornamental techniques together were:

Corbel bracket in the mansion of Wu Yinsun, the Intendant of Circuit in Yangzhou.

Corbel bracket in Ruiguang Pagoda in Suzhou.

The Integration of Decorative and Practical Purposes

Most of the ornamentation in traditional Chinese architecture were not merely accessories, but served practical purposes as an integral part of the building structures. These adornments were not aesthetically pleasing but also suited to the nature of the building materials and in line with the logic of mechanics.

Let us take the roof beam of the traditional timber framework as an example. A type of curved beams, known as "crescent beams" (with the central portions arching upwards) helped to disperse the load of the roofs from the building structures, and thus prevented the roofs from drooping, and also created sturdy-looking sculpts. Many vernacular dwellings liked to have ornamental carvings on both the protruding ends of the crescent beams, and some even carved the sharp beaks of cranes, fish scales or dragons' heads along the contours of the beams, integrating the curves with animal motifs and other patterns considered auspicious by the Chinese.

Most of the wooden columns or pillars were round shaped, and were thick in the middle and slimmer at both ends. These columns were not built perpendicular to the ground, but slightly tilted at the top, to fulfill the logic of mechanics as well as correct optical illusion, such that the structures appeared more stable. To prevent the building columns from rotting, column bases often

Partition door.

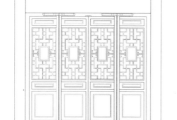

Wooden partition.

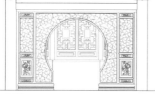

comprised stone carved in the shapes of drums, round baskets and vases, while designs ranging from simple patterns to plants and animals were sculpted onto the bodies of the columns.

Corbel brackets, known as *dougong* are a unique feature in classical Chinese architecture. Each set of brackets was made up of tiers of outstretching arms cushioned with square blocks called *dou* and *sheng*, rectangular *gong*, and diagonal *ang*. By inserting the brackets into the column heads, these brackets provided support for the projecting eaves and thus multi-tiered roofs of the buildings by transferring the load to the base of the columns. The complicated structures were similar to the modern day grid structures and had become focal points as they were visually pleasing.

Before the use of glass, the windows of classical buildings were constructed using paper or translucent materials such as ground fish scales and seashells. The lattice window panels were densely patterned to adequately shelter the building interiors against bad weather. The ancient Chinese built upon the design of the lattice panels by decorating them with compositions of all sorts, including patterns, calligraphy, plant and animal motifs.

It was the common practice of the ancient Chinese to lend a dignified air to any architecture of great importance by building them on high podiums, such as the three main halls of the Forbidden City in Beijing, which were built on three-storey high podiums. Bas-relief of all types of plant and animal motifs were carved onto the frames of the balustrade surrounding the podium and the ornamental column heads, creating a podium that is opulent and vivid in appearance.

Much of traditional Chinese architecture is intrinsically beautiful. Ancient Chinese craftsmen simply added decorative details which conformed to the building structures and practicalities of design.

The Differentiation of Social Classes

In the ancient Chinese feudalistic society, the Confucian concept of "*li*" reign supreme in categorizing society into various class levels, with regards to all matters, including architecture and

Gargoyles in the shape of dragon's heads in Taihe Hall, the Forbidden City, Beijing.

Crescent beams.

133

architectural ornamentation. As a result, the construction of architecture was based on the premises of aesthetics as well one's social status, which would then denote the types of ornamentation, colors, quality of materials and themes that a person was entitled to using.

During the Ming Dynasty, common civilians were prevented by law from using corbel brackets and colorful ornamentation. Hence, corbel brackets were mainly used in palaces, courts, places of religious worship and residences of high-rank officials and thus became a symbol of the strict standards for the stratification of social classes.

Bright colors and colorful paintings were the basic elements in classifying the social class under which a particular architecture was grouped under and consequently, the social background of the owner. The colors of rooftops were the most important; roofs with yellow-glazed tiles were considered the most sacred as these tiles were only used for buildings specially designated by the emperors, such as the Confucius Temple. All the buildings within the grounds of the imperial palaces, with very few exceptions of special requests, were roofed with yellow-glazed tiles. Temples, other royal and official residences used yellowish-green, green and greenish-gray colored tiles respectively. Civilians were the lowest among the ranks and were permitted to use only grey-colored roof tiles. As for the colors of walls, the walls of main buildings were painted red while the wooden structures of supplementary buildings were painted green, and vernacular dwellings and gardens were using red, green, brown, and black together.

The main purpose of oil paintings in classic Chinese architecture was to protect

Oil painting in the Long Corridor in the Summer Palace. This oil painting depicts "The Matchmaking for Mu Guiying".

the timber structures from the corrosive effects of the weather. Paintings were depicted on all the structures of the buildings, including the ridgepole, corbel brackets and ceilings. The colors used in the depictions range from the main colors of different shades of green, to gold, red and black, and to differentiate people's class by if they use gold and the pattern of dragon and how much they use. During the Qing Dynasty, colorful depictions were also included on most of the architecture in the imperial palaces, temples and official courts. Artists had a free rein in the range of subjects when painting for residences and gardens, which included stories of heroes, landscapes, flowers, and animals. For example, the 8,000 oil paintings in the long corridor in the Summer Palace contain the scenes from classic literatures such as *Dream of the Red Chamber*, *Journey to the West*, *Romance of Three Kingdoms*, and *Outlaws of the Marsh*, and others.

Since time in memorial, the front gates of a building had always been a symbol of the social and financial status of an

The red golden-knobbed gate in the Imperial Palace.

Different forms of roof in ancient China represent different classes of buildings.

The Chinese character "fu" (happiness) was surrounded by four bats (share the same pronunciation with fu *in Chinese).*

individual. The gates to a person's residence would have to be in line with his social status, from the sturdiest and most hefty gates of the imperial palaces to the common civilian's simple wooden gates. Even architectural details such as the number of nails in the gates (the more nails there were, the higher the status of the individual), the colors of the gates (from high to low are red, green, and black,) and the types of metals used for the door-knockers (from high to low are copper, tin, and iron), represented class differences.

The Symbolic Meaning of Ornamentation

Traditional Chinese architecture possessed the outstanding characteristic of integrating Chinese philosophies and aesthetic values together through the use of symbolic representations in the form of wordplay (such as homonyms) or visual metaphors.

In general, structural components in classic Chinese architecture were created out of necessity with ornamentation added for their symbolic meanings rather than for the mere sake of aesthetic beauty.

Someone once mentioned that, "Chinese architecture is about the art of rooftop designs". These words fully reflect the strong visual impressions that the large rooftops found in Chinese architecture etched upon many people. There are indeed many ornamental rooftop elements which greatly enhanced the roof silhouettes.

The ridge of a house served the purpose of protecting the intersecting areas of different bays from exposure to water damage. Located at the curved ends of the roof's ridge were ornamental pottery figures known as *zhengwen* (animal's mouth) or *chiwei* (owl's tail) which served as totems guarding against fire. Other auspicious animals found on the ridges included immortals, dragons, phoenixes etc.. Some other figures possessed symbolic meanings such as family harmony, prosperity and protective purposes against natural disasters.

The carvings and pictorial depictions found on other parts of the architecture similarly contained many visual metaphors which reflected the people's desire for auspicious outcomes as well as traditions and customs. Examples included the use of animal motifs such as the mythical dragon, which symbolized the emperor, the lion as a symbol of great strength and the green dragon, white tiger, red bird and black union of tortoise and snake, which were representative of the cardinal directions, east, south, west and north. An example of the use of homonyms would be the depiction of four bats (*bian fu* in Chinese, sounding the same as *fu*, the Chinese character which represents good fortune or happiness) surrounding the Chinese character, *fu*, to symbolize good fortune in the Chinese saying, " *wu fu lin men*", that is, all happiness come into the house.

Differences in Ornamentation Due to Historical, Regional and Ethnical Backgrounds

The dynastic cycles of China played a part in defining the styles of architectural ornamentation in classic Chinese architecture, as old artistic techniques were refined upon, and new design elements were created and incorporated over the centuries. The architectural style of the Han Dynasty had been described as serious and sturdy, the Tang Dynasty's architectural style was bright and generous, while Song Dynasty possessed fluid and lively styles; and the styles of the Ming and Qing Dynasties were dignified and opulent. The chief subject matters depicted in ornamentation also differed from dynasty to dynasty, with for example, the emphasis on the depictions of animal motifs during the Zhou and Shang dynasties, heroes, immortals, and banquets during Qin and Han dynasties, lotus motifs, Buddhist artifacts, dance parties, and exotic things during Sui and Tang dynasties, flowers, animals, folk stories, and legends in Song and Yuan dynasties, and all themes and topics in Ming and Qing Dynasties.

Geographical factors such as differences in the natural environment and weather also contributed to the differences in architectural styles. The harsh, chilly weather conditions on the Qinghai-Tibet Plateau meant that high-walled stone buildings were a pragmatic choice for most people. The decoration of the buildings was chiefly reflected in the walls which were stuffed with hemp. On the other hand, the weather in southern China is mainly hot, humid and wet. As such, maximizing air circulation is an important outcome of the local architectural style, seen through the construction of large windows and doors for rooms facing the inner courtyards and sky wells.

Every ethnic group has its own distinctive artistic styles, infused with cultural elements with regards to architecture. For instance, the Tibetans prefer the use of bold, contrasting colors, gold engravings, intricate pictorial depictions and carved wooden window and door panels; the Uighurs excel in the making of wooden

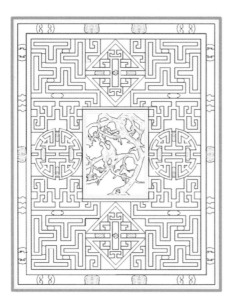

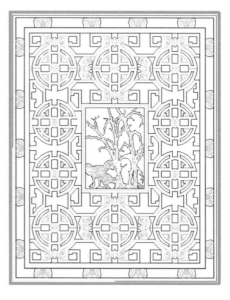

Latticed window with animal images, the patterns are parrot (top left), peacock (top right), crane (bottom left), chicken (bottom right).

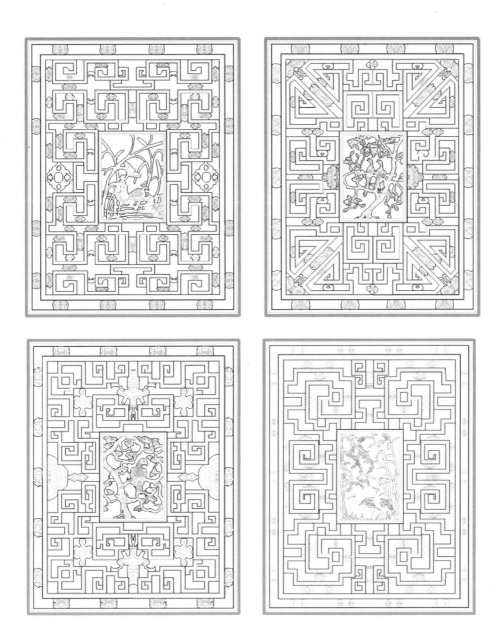

Latticed window with animal images, the patterns are mandarin duck (top left), pie (top right), hawk (bottom left), double cranes (bottom right).

139

The ceiling ornamentation of Tian'an Gate.

sculptures, plaster ornaments and glazed tiles; the Bai people like to paste bricks on the wall; the Dai people usually use bamboo ornamentation on their bamboo buildings; and the Hui people put much attention to carving and colorful painting on bricks and timbers.

The highly varied styles of architectural ornamentation have deeply enriched the overall artistry of classic Chinese architecture. With the integration of many subjects including ethnicity, topography, religions, philosophies, ethic, folk customs, history, and society, architectural ornamentation played an important role in shaping the uniqueness of ancient Chinese architecture.

The ornamentation on the top of columns of Uygur building in Kashgar, Xinjiang.

The Design and Construction of Ancient Chinese Architecture

The execution of architectural design and construction in ancient China was extremely similar to what is being carried out today. The project overseer would place great emphasis on surveying the land and also made use of construction blueprints as well as miniature models. Over a long period of practice, the Chinese building craftsmen had developed three-dimensional architectural drawings (similar to axonometric drawings in modern times) to oversee the actual construction. After the Han Dynasty, architectural drawings and explanatory documents were mandatory by law for any large-scale construction projects. By the 10th Century AD, the use of architectural drawings had reached a highly sophisticated level.

As an illustration of the use of architectural drawings, during the Sui Dynasty, the master architect, Yuwen Kai, compiled a detailed report regarding his onsite survey for the construction of Mingtang. The approval of the emperor was finally obtained through his delivery of a detailed architectural drawing and model for the building project.

For more than 2,000 years (since the beginning of the Zhou Dynasty), offices had been specially designated for architectural development, and officials of construction were put in charged of portfolios such as design, construction and the distribution of building materials. The set-up of these offices ensured the highly efficient distribution of labor and materials, which in turn led to the standardization and modularization of building components for classic Chinese architecture on a large scale.

By the Ming Dynasty, the Chinese system of architectural design and building had become highly advanced. All the various government projects were managed and executed by the specially setup labor management unit. The rulers of the Qing Dynasty brought the setup of the architectural and design unit one step further, with the implementation of two departments, namely, the finance department which was in charged of financial planning and budgeting for construction materials, and the design department which was responsible for devising architectural drafts, made-to-scale drawings and building models for guiding actual construction. One of the most outstanding craftsmen during the Qing Dynasty was Lei Fada (1619–1693), who, together with his descendants, oversaw the imperial architectural department for eight generations. During their tenure of more than 200 years, they oversaw the completion of many major building projects such as Old Summer Palace, Qingyi Palace, Rehe Palace, Chang Mausoleum and Hui Mausoleum.

Mingtang, the place for emperors to give lectures.

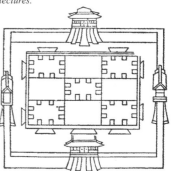

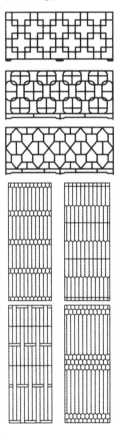

The lattice window and balustrade in Yuan Ye (Gardening).

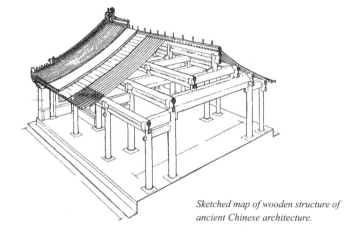

Sketched map of wooden structure of ancient Chinese architecture.

The establishment of the timber framework of ancient Chinese architecture also brought about the standardization of construction methods and modularization of building components. Compiled in 1091, the imperial architectural manual, *yingzao fashi*, provided a detailed summary of the building experiences of the previous generations, and standardized construction components for all wooden structures according to eight different grades of measurements. Once the size of a particular building was fixed, a standard set of fixed measurements for all the various components followed suit. It was, therefore, the effective modularization of construction components which enabled effective building techniques to be passed on through the ages, all the way up to the Qing Dynasty.

Once the precise measurements for each building component had been standardized, the wooden components could be manufactured in advance without the need to take into account the size of the land area slated for construction. Consequently, the quantities of materials and amount of labor required to complete any architectural project could be accurately calculated in advance, by basing requirements on made-to-scale architectural drawings and models. Overall, modularization had led to the effective financial budgeting, management and execution of many building projects.

Western Influences on Chinese Architecture

The relic of Western-style buildings in Old Summer Palace in Beijing.

Before the Opium war in 1840, classic Chinese architecture, which had the highly sophisticated timber framework as its foundation and also possessed unique and sequential styles, had almost no contact with Western architecture. A few Western-style buildings did exist, including the churches and shops built by the Portuguese who settled in Macao in 1557, the buildings erected by the Thirteen Hongs in Guangzhou after 1685, as well as the earlier mentioned European-style buildings located in Old Summer Palace in Beijing. However, these western-style buildings were neither widespread nor created an extensive influence on Chinese architecture.With the invasion of colonialism and imperialism, the collapse of the feudalistic economic structure and the development of capitalism in China after the Opium War, Western architectural styles began to have a widespread influence. The architectural styles and technologies of the modern times began to appear in China one after another, creating a new architectural system for modern China, whereby the old and new systems co-existed. This also led to a merging of Chinese and Western architectural styles. Apparently, the development of the Chinese architectural system of the modern times was not a progressive evolution of the traditional Chinese timber framework, but a direct outcome brought about by historical conditions, namely, the invasion of China by the Western imperialist powers. As a result, buildings defined by the new system of architecture were mainly built in few large cities, especially treaty ports or cities occupied by a single foreign concession. From these areas, the new architectural styles gradually spread to other parts of China. From the latter half of the 19th century up to the 1930s, European and American architecture underwent a period of transformation from neoclassicism and romanticism to eclecticism and the new arts movement, and then to modern architecture. All these architectural styles were eventually featured, either on their own or in an inter-play of styles in the semi-feudal, semi-colonized cities of modern China. In the cities occupied by multiple foreign concessions such as Shanghai, Tianjin and Hankou, the city landscapes were more heterogeneous, with a mixture of then popular architectural styles from Europe and the United States. Due to the presence of unified city planning, cities dominated by single imperialist powers such as Qingdao, Dalian and Harbin possessed a more harmonious integration of architectural styles.

European-style building in the mansion of Wu Yinsun, the Intendant of Circuit in Yangzhou. It was used to welcome foreign guests.

Night scene of Shanghai Bund.

Western-style buildings in Shanghai Bund.

Shanghai

Shanghai remains the most important city with the greatest influence in the modern architectural history of China. Following the opening up of Shanghai as a commercial port, Western architects as well as Western-trained Chinese architects introduced the culture of Western architecture to the city. Hence, from the second half of the 19th Century up to the early 20th Century, these architects built a large number of buildings that were artistically brilliant and functionally effective, and also represented a complete departure from the traditional Chinese architectural system and its concept of architectural space. In Shanghai, modern buildings with architectural styles representative of almost all historical periods could be found. Architectural styles range from ancient Egyptian, the classical pillars of the Greco-Roman era, Byzantine, Roman, Russian Orthodox, Gothic, Renaissance, Baroque, Classical and Neoclassical to the styles of modern architectural schools of thoughts, as well as traditional Chinese palatial-style and folk architecture. As such, Shanghai could be described as a vivid historical account of the architectural styles of the world. At the same time, these modern buildings also reflected regional styles from countries all over the world, including Britain, Germany,

France, Italy, Spain, the Mediterranean region, the United States, India, Japan, Russia, Northern Europe and Islamic nations. Some of these regional styles were embodied in the overall look of the buildings, while others were featured in the use of decorative patterns, colors and details.The origins of the development of Shanghai as a metropolis in recent times could be traced to the Bund—itself a microcosm of Shanghai, and hence a symbol of the city's development. The architecture of the Bund has undergone three pivotal phases in history, namely the birth of modern architectural forms during the mid 19th Century, the era of great prosperity of the late 19th Century and early 20th Century, and the flourishing 1920s and 1930s. Up till today, 52 buildings showcasing various architectural styles including Gothic, Baroque, Roman, Classical, the Renaissance and a mixture of the East and West, still lined the west side of the Bund. Buildings most representative of the architecture on the Bund are the Bank of China, the Peace Hotel, the Customs House and the Hong Kong and Shanghai Bank. Although the works of different architects with varied styles, the architectural styles of these buildings still integrate seamlessly to etch out a beautiful skyline along the west coast of the Huangpu River, and thus renowned as "the exhibition of the architecture of 10,000 countries".

Tianjin

A short distance away from the political epicenter of Beijing, Tianjin's proximity to the capital city is a crucial factor for its recent city development. In Tianjin after 1860, several countries including England, France, the United States, Germany, Japan, Russia, Austria, Italy, and Belgium established foreign concessions respectively. In fact, in Asia, the only foreign concessions established by Italy, Belgium and Austria were to be found in Tianjin, hence marking the city's unique position in the modern history of the world.Building activities were carried out in the foreign concessions on a large scale, from 1900 to 1937, and especially from 1912 to 1937, with a multitude of architectural types and styles "flooding" the scene within a short period of time. Due to the impact of the First World War, some foreign concessions remained for only a short period of time and hence did not create much of an impact, while other foreign powers like England and France continued to expand their areas of influence, especially in the prosperous areas of Zhongjie Street and Quan Ye Department Store where building activities were congregated.The first street to be established in the Anglo-French Concession, Zhongjie Street (now renamed Jiefang North Road) was known as "the Street of the Banks", given the large number of banks built there. Many of these buildings showcased neoclassic architectural styles, in the use of classical pillars; with an emphasis on symmetry and axis, and the relationship between principal and

Western-style house in Five Grand Avenues in Tianjin.

subordinate features strictly adhered to, creating architectural compositions with precise proportions, which were elegant and opulent in styles. Classic examples include the Hong Kong and Shanghai Bank (1925) and the Yokohama Specie Bank (1926). The commercial center of Tianjin eventually shifted to the area of the Quan Ye Department Store, located in the French concession after 1900. During the 1920s, there was rapid commercial development in this area, with a large number of commercial and entertainment complexes built, such as shops, hotels, restaurants and theatres. Quickly overtaking the old city area in terms of prosperity and commercial activities from 1922, landmark buildings built successively in the Quan Ye Department Store area included the National Grand Hotel (1922), the National Commercial Bank (1925), the Hui Zhong Hotel (1928) and the Quan Ye Department Store (1928). Although erected during the same time as the banks in Zhongjie Street, the architectural styles of these commercial buildings differed greatly from the "strict" styles of the banks. In the Quan Ye Department Store area, buildings were created in a multitude of shapes and sizes, and featured a mixture of architectural styles influenced by modern architectural schools of thought. An example of this fluid style would be the building of tall towers to maximize commercial advertising effects.

Qingdao

Qingdao began to thrive as a city during the modern times. During the initial 20 to 30 years of its development, it was reduced to a colony under German rule and then Japanese rule subsequently, before it was finally taken back by the Chinese government.The basic layout of Qingdao as a modern city was mapped out by the German colonial government in 1900, and was clearly influenced by then popular European urban city planning concepts of "zonal city" and "garden-style residence". Taking into consideration the topography of the island city, the colonial government devised networks of roads and buildings according to the make-up of the natural coastal lines and mountainous terrain to advocate the picturesque, lively and carefree styles of city-planning in European cities during the turn of the 20th Century.Although the Germans ruled Qingdao for less than 20 years, they left behind a great legacy of Bavarian-style architectural buildings. The city center of the Qingdao region, with a central axis measuring 200 meters, was located on the foot of the southern slope of Guanhaishan Hill. Located on the northern end of the city center was the Governor's Office while the Joeskee Memorial Tower could be found on the sea bay located on

Seaside villa in Qingdao Badaguan.

Granite Mansion, former German governor-general's villa in Qingdao.

the southern end. Surrounding the city center were landmark buildings such as the Jiao'ao Court of Law (1912), the British Consulate (1907), the Hotel Wirtshaus Fur Katz and the Hotel Prinz Heinrich (1911). At the same time, there were also buildings based on the new Renaissance architectural styles of Germany, including the Qingdao Railway Station (1902), Jiao'ao Police Station (1905), Jiao'ao Post Office (1910) and the Deutsch-Asiatische Bank (1906). The "Red House" bore the style of the New Arts Movement while the Beach Hotel (1904), with its bare wooden framework and the Marine Club (1899) were also important landmarks under German rule.Built in 1906, the German governor-general's office was the grandest building of that era, possessing specific baroque-style elements as well as Windsor-style rooftops. On the other hand, the Governor's Villa (as known as the Granite Mansion, 1906) and the Governor's Residence (1908) were built in styles, quite different from Bavarian architecture of the same period, with their granite facades and complicated layouts of overlapping rooftops. Architectural buildings which had the greatest impact on the overall look of Qingdao could be attributed to the stand alone mansions built during the German rule. The prevalent school of thought in Europe then was architectural design inspired by the Art Deco movement, which resulted in the popularity of garden-style residences. On top of the preference for garden-style residences, the mansions also reflected the individual owners' tastes, leading to the proliferation of mansions with half-timber structures, colonial-style mansions, neoclassic structures and gothic-style residences. Mansions built in the area of Badaguan were most representative of the myriad of styles employed during that period. More than a hundred residential mansions from that era can still be found in the area of Badaguan today. These houses stand apart, and yet seem to congregate at the same time, dotting undulating, hilly terrain and forming a breathtaking portrait of red tiles, yellow walls, green trees and mountains, blue sea and azure sky.

Dalian

Located at the southern tip of the Liaodong Peninsula, Dalian is the hub of marine traffic in Northern China, and therefore has critical economic and military importance due to its strategic geographical location. In 1898, Dalian became a czarist-Russian concession and henceforth began its journey as a modernizing colonial city. In 1905, Japan invaded and occupied Dalian, speeding up the process of colonizing the city all the way up to the end of the WWII in 1945. The architectural development of Dalian could be divided into three phases. In the earliest phase, the czarist-Russian regime established the basic structure and layout of the city according to the Russian city structure of central squares with avenues radiating outwards, thus creating a city

European-style blocks in Dalian.

151

reflecting Russian and European as well as eclectic styles. At the same time, Russian folk architecture of wooden structures also appeared in Dalian, with the building of intricate little wooden houses topped with green-colored turrets, covered with feather-shaped tiles. An example of the eclectic style of architecture would be the business school set up during that era, which incorporated the mountain flower motifs of Greece and Roman colonnades. The Japanese regime continued to build upon the foundation of the Russian regime's urban planning scheme, replicating European and American classical architectural designs for buildings to spruce up the large Square and hasten urban development. Around the Large Square, examples of historical landmarks which shaped the second phase of urban development in Dalian, included the Dalian Civil Administration Office (Dalian Foreign Trade and Economic Cooperation Bureau today) with its Gothic-revivalist architectural style, the Yokohama Specie Bank decked out in Renaissance style of the later period (Bank of China today), the Yamato Hotel with its Renaissance style (Dalian Hotel today) and the Bank of Korean of the Classical-revivalist style (The People's Bank of China today). As the Japanese regime continued with its further military invasion of China, Dalian was regarded as the base for its expansionist strategy and thus more efforts were put into developing and increasing urban planning. During the late 1920s, Japan was increasingly influenced by popular, modern German architectural schools of thought. During

European-style building in downtown Dalian.

the 1930s, the adoption of these German styles by the leading Japanese architects in Dalian led to the creation of many buildings which were examples of international architectural styles, interspersed with natural and fluid elements of Japanese design. Henceforth, the development of these architectural styles had the greatest impact upon the overall look of Dalian city and also marked the third phase in the city's modern architectural history.

Harbin

Harbin was founded as a city in 1898, by the czarist Russian regime which was constructing the Trans-Siberian Railroad across northeastern China. As a result of its special historical background, a unique urban architectural culture comprising a blend of traditional Russian folk architecture, old and modern Western-style architecture and traditional Chinese architecture was created.

The planning of the urban city layout of Harbin commenced in 1899. It was modeled after Russia's capital city, Moscow, whereby the city was divided into several districts by the inter-crossing T-shaped railway tracks. Many of the historical buildings showcasing traditional Russian architecture and the designs of the new Art Deco Movement were built on China Street in Butou District (now Central Street in Daoli District), including the Concord Bank (1917), the Modern Hotel (1913), Qiu Lin Business Shop (1919) and the Russian Immigrants' Association (1909). Built in 1903, the Harbin Railway Station served as the gateway to the city and was a landmark in its own right, with its New Art Deco design elements.

The Russian Orthodox Church played an important role in shaping the unique city landscape of Harbin. As early as 1898, the St. Nicola Cathedral of the Orthodox faith was built upon the Southern Peak, the highest point in Harbin. The cathedral was laid out in the shape of the Greek cross and was built according to the traditional Russian wooden structure with tent-like, octagonal–shaped roofs topped with onion-shaped domes. Once hailed as the symbol of the "Moscow of the East", the St. Nicola Cathedral had since been demolished. Up until the 1930s, the number of Orthodox Churches in Harbin had increased to 25. Built from 1923 to 1932, the St. Sophia Cathedral was the largest Orthodox Church in Harbin. Its design was chiefly defined by the Byzantine architectural style with the use of brick arches, and its floor layout, in the shape of the Latin cross, had the highest points at each end sheltered by tent-like roofs topped with onion-shaped domes. The highest point at the intersection of the cross-shaped layout was then topped by a giant onion-shaped dome, which thus functioned as the core structure of the cathedral, lending it an aura of magnificence akin to the St. Sophia Cathedral of Constantinople. It is still the visual highlight for visitors in Harbin today.

The largest church in the Far East—St. Sophia Cathedral in Harbin.

153

Appendix: A Brief Chronology of China

Xia Dynasty	2070–1600 BC
Shang Dynasty	1600–1046 BC
Zhou Dynasty	1066–256 BC
Spring and Autumn Period	770–476 BC
Warring States Period	475–221 BC
Qin Dynasty	221–206 BC
Western Han Dynasty	206 BC–AD 8
Eastern Han Dynasty	25–220
Three Kingdoms	220–280
Western Jin Dynasty	265–317
Eastern Jin Dynasty	317–420
Southern and Northern Dynasties	420–589
Sui Dynasty	581–618
Tang Dynasty	618–907
Five Dynasties	907–960
Northern Song Dynasty	960–1127
Southern Song Dynasty	1127–1279
Yuan Dynasty	1271–1368
Ming Dynasty	1368–1644
Qing Dynasty	1644–1911